Vital for Everyone's Success, Happiness, and Fulfillment

I'm
Fired Up
for a
Better
Life

**Re-Energize, Go for That Dream,
and Empower Others to Do the Same**

Anne Whiting

A *Possibility Press* Book

Dedication

To my loving husband, Spencer, and everyone who wants a happier, more meaningful, successful, and fulfilling life.

Acknowledgment

I'm grateful for all the encouragement and help I received from so many people in making this book a reality, especially the editors at Possibility Press. The rest of you know who you are. Thank you so much. You're the BEST.

Published by *Possibility Press*
PossibilityPress.com

Manufactured in the United States of America

Contents

	Welcome—It's Time to Get Fired Up for a Better Life	5
1.	A Better Life Begins as Soon as You Get Fired Up for It	11
2.	Negative Self-Talk Can Douse Your Fire	16
3.	What Do You Really Want?	21
4.	What Are Your Favorite Activities?	27
5.	Use Your Imagination to Fire Up Your Desire for a Better Life	31
6.	Have Any Myths About Success?	36
7.	Vision, Mission, and Purpose	45
8.	Putting It All Together	53
9.	The Dream Fires You Up to Take Action and Succeed	58
10.	Build Your Business or Profession to Live a Better Life	63
11.	Make the Most of Your Resources	69
12.	What About Money?	75
13.	Make Each Day Count	82
14.	Upgrade Your Vitality	89
15.	Maintaining a Positive Attitude Is Essential for a Better Life	93
16.	Creating Affirmations to Support Your Dream for a Better Life	101
17.	Putting Your Affirmations into Action	108
18.	Persist Until You Achieve...Then Keep on Going?	111
19.	Paint Your Picture of Success	117
20.	Avoid Dream-Delaying Hooks	123
21.	Stay Fired Up to Go and Grow	127
22.	27 Tips for Staying Fired Up for a Better Life	132
23.	Now Go Out and Make a Bigger Difference	148
	I'm Fired Up for a Better Life—The Creed	159
	Who Is Anne Whiting?	160

Being fired up for a better life is not meant to be just a temporary state of excitement. It's a foundational attitude for enhancing your life, so maintaining it is essential for greater success, happiness, and fulfillment. As you make the fired-up state of mind an enduring part of your character your life continues getting better, and you energize those around you.

Be fired up as you share the benefits that can be derived from the product, service, or opportunity you're offering... then watch others get excited!

Welcome

It's Time to Get Fired Up for a Better Life

"Whatever you can do or dream, you can begin it.
Boldness has genius, power and magic in it. Begin it now."
Goethe

As a child you had dreams, didn't you? You were excited about life and wanted to do something special and believed you would do it. But what happened to those dreams when you grew up? Have you kept them alive or let someone who's probably unsure of themselves put-down your desires or dissuade you from pursuing them?

Have you finally reached the point where you're truly yearning for your life, or at least some aspect of it, to improve? Or if you're satisfied with your life just as it is right now, might you still have some other objectives, be they big or small, that you'd like to accomplish? Inside you are all the talent seeds you need to make that happen. You have a unique gift in yourself to share with the world, and only *you* can live it and be who you were meant to be. There's only one you.

Following the Crowd Is a Dead End—It Won't Better Your Life

This often unconscious choice doesn't enable anyone to better his or her life. After all, in the long-run, the average-thinking person doesn't do all that well. It's only those who break away from the pack and embrace their own uniqueness who can truly go beyond the crowd-imposed limits of everyday sameness.

Children's dreams are often BIG and seem totally possible and easy to them since they're open-minded, full of wonder, and optimistic. For most kids the sky's the limit, but their fire often gets doused or dampened by any discouragement they're exposed to growing up. Narrow-minded, short-sighted, negative-thinking role models and nay-saying peers, all of whom are stuck in rut of miserable complacency, can shut kids down; programming them for mediocrity.

If any of that happens, which is all too common, dreams are unfortunately too easily put aside and forgotten. The child becomes an adult who typically leads a common everyday existence... just getting by. Surrounded by others who are doing the same, they get lulled into believing "That's just the way it is." They resign themselves to staying stuck right where they are, or even letting things get worse, not believing they can do anything about it.

They may long for a better life, but they don't do anything different to make it so, continuing the typical so-so (same old same old) saga of hanging-in-there. In the hopes of striking it rich, they may buy lottery tickets and play games of chance. But that doesn't change anything except to lighten of their wallet of money that could have been more wisely spent on something else, like paying down debt. Instead of getting ahead, they're falling further behind.

Challenges Can Be Our Best Teachers

Many live day-to-day with a sense of resignation, believing they have to take whatever life dishes out. But it doesn't have to be that way. Unfortunately, there are those who wait until they experience a crisis or major challenge of some sort, before they stop and look at how their lives have been going. They wake up one day, realizing that something's missing, and start to admit that they're bored with the same old routine. Deep down inside it's something that may have been gnawing at them for years.

Rest assured, your life can be improved and, as time goes on, you can also achieve other aspirations... whatever you may envision. It's up to you. Others have done it, and you can too.

Throughout my childhood, I experienced crisis after crisis. When I was six, my mother became seriously ill, constantly in and out of the hospital for the next 15 years, until she passed away. Alcoholism was a constant presence in the family; and like most children living in that kind of environment, I grew up insecure and scared. When I was in my late 20s, I nearly married an alcoholic. I learned a lot from those experiences. I got the help I needed through therapy, personal growth workshops, and recovery support groups, becoming a stronger adult as a result.

As I learned and grew, I broke free of the past. I know now that those crises were blessings in disguise, for they taught me compassion and understanding, which developed into strength, courage, perseverance, and faith. I've been blessed with the support of others in overcoming negativity, and empowered to step forward in continuously making my dreams come true. This has all helped keep me going and growing, and remain essential parts of my life.

As a child, I dreamed of becoming a teacher, helping others, and being happily married. Growing older, other dreams surfaced as I wanted to do even more, from starting my own business to writing books. Those dreams defined my life's direction, and helped enable and sustain me in my quest to achieve them.

Have there been times when you've broken free from the bonds of the past and succeeded, even when it seemed nearly impossible? I'll bet there have. For example, some people have had such experiences during athletic or sporting events, where they've set new records or exceeded their personal best. Many others have worked through challenges which, in the overcoming, strengthened and enabled them to advance in their jobs, businesses, or professions, resulting in their improving their lives.

Do you remember what it was like the first time you achieved a major goal or helped someone overcome a challenge? It felt great, didn't it? Did you ever throw a surprise birthday party for someone you love? These things got you fired up, and when you're fired up, more exciting things happen and people want to be around you.

Create More of the Life You Want

What about your childhood dreams? Are you living them? If not, do you still want to? Or, do you have newer dreams that are equally or more important to you, but maybe you're not quite sure where to start in achieving them? Once you're working toward your dreams, old or new, big or small, you begin gaining momentum in creating more of the life you want. You're on an upward spiral.

As a speaker and trainer, I've seen amazing things happen to people when they get fired up, while striving for their special dreams and goals. When people believe in themselves, get fired up, and start taking action, amazing things can occur. I've witnessed case after case of people overcoming obstacles, propelled by their dreams, succeeding against all odds.

This can happen for you too. You have the power and ability to make your dreams come true. But while you may have the most splendid of dreams, they'll just remain "Someday I'll..." wishes until you get fired up, stay fired up, and focus on making them realities. Otherwise, "Someday" becomes a disappointing new word called "Never."

Can You Really Make a Bigger Difference?

Yes! Being fired up for a better life can also help you make a bigger difference in the world around you and beyond, as you keep going and growing, expanding your sphere of influence. You're a distinctive human being who can touch the lives of others in special ways; and you're probably already making a difference perhaps in ways of which you're unaware, just by being kind and caring.

The Birth of *I'm Fired Up for a Better Life*

I love watching people improve their lives as they move on their dreams—it's so inspiring. Everyone who does so is like a match lighting kindling. Many years ago when the dreams inside of me were set ablaze, I learned that my deepest fulfillment and meaning came from helping others take action on *their* dreams. I love to watch people grow.

Over the years, I've discovered that while almost everyone would like to have a better life, very few actually create it. Since there's no training in school about identifying, believing in, nurturing, and realizing dreams, most people don't know what actions to take or *how* to follow through and succeed in making them come true. Far too many people die "with their music still in them, their song unsung." But it doesn't have to be that way.

Now is the time to get fired up and start working toward achieving your dreams for a better life, big or small. Associate with positive people, including fine role models who've blazed the path before you. Enthusiastically follow—no, chase—your dreams, letting nothing and no one stand in your way. Pursue them and they'll take you where you're meant to go... as long as you get fired up, stay fired up, and keep taking action.

When you're fired up for a better life, you create the atmosphere for great things to happen... even miracles! Believe you can achieve more than you may now think possible. I hope this book helps you get fired up to overcome any obstacles you may have let stop you in the past. It has tools, techniques, and stories of ordinary people, just like you and me, who overcame their challenges and bettered their lives. Their experiences are shared to inspire and support you in bettering *yours* as well, whatever that may mean for you.

Since you undoubtedly desire to have more success, prosperity, happiness, and perhaps even more friends, keep reading. Maybe you want to be more financially secure so you can spend more time with your family, traveling and doing other things you love to do. Your new future begins today. You *can* do whatever it takes to achieve your objectives, starting with the decision to do so.

I'm thankful for the lessons God has taught me in the creation of this book, and I hope it'll help you on your quest to be fired up for improving your life.

It's Time to Get Fired Up for a Better Life

Inside of you is the fire of life. It's your passion, your purpose, your mission, and your fulfillment, all of which give more meaning to your life. It ignites and burns brightly when you're doing whatever it takes to create the life you want. When you're fired up, your fire can warm those who get close to you and ignite *their* fire. This can excite them to join you and get fired up for better lives of their own... and on down the line. As Helen Keller said, *"Alone we can do so little; together we can do so much."*

When you're fired up you start feeling stronger, vibrantly alive, and more courageous. You start believing you can overcome any obstacle and meet any challenge head-on... and win. You start believing you can achieve what may have seemed impossible to you in the past. You start believing you can live the life you want.

You *can* have more happiness and success than you may have ever imagined. It all starts inside you—with your fire. The choice is yours. The time to start improving your life is now!

Are you fired up for a better life, re-energized to go for that dream, and willing to empower others to do the same? I'll bet you are. So let's get started...

Onward and upward to your better life,
Anne

The 32 Principles of
I'm Fired Up for a Better Life

1. Choose and Commit to Success
2. Dream-Build Often
3. Pursuing a Better Life Makes a Difference in the World Around You
4. Get Absolutely Clear About What You Really, Really Want
5. Use Your Imagination
6. Uncover Your Myths About Success
7. Identify Role Models
8. Read Positive Books, Listen to Motivational/Educational Audios, and Attend Seminars
9. Act "As If"... with Enthusiasm
10. Take Action and Keep Moving
11. Have a Solid Plan
12. Capture Your Creativity
13. Use Your Resources
14. Connect with the Right People
15. Manage Your Money and Get Out of Debt
16. Use Your Time Wisely
17. Take Care of Your Health
18. Laugh About It
19. Your Dream for a Better Life Can Help You Recover...
20. Go from "It Could Happen" to "It Will Happen!"
21. Don't Be Unattached to Any Particular Person or Outcome
22. Be Patient
23. Learn from Your Mistakes and Keep Going
24. Cultivate an Attitude of Gratitude
25. Use Affirmations Daily to Get and Stay Fired Up
26. Use Action Options to Get and Stay Fired Up
27. Finish What You Start
28. Create a Dream Collage
29. Let the Child Inside Your Heart Come Out and Play
30. Avoid the Hooks
31. Do What Winners Do to Stay Fired Up
32. Make a Bigger Difference

Chapter 1

A Better Life Begins as Soon as You Get Fired Up for It

Belief Is the Fuel that Enables It to Happen

"There is a real magic in enthusiasm. It spells the difference between mediocrity and accomplishment."
Norman Vincent Peale

Y ou uniquely reveal and share your enthusiasm when you're fired up, which increases your potential to live the life you want, while affecting others' lives in positive ways.

Whatever you have or haven't done up until now is in the past. Whatever you do with the rest of your life starts today, right now, in the present moment; and the *present* is a gift you give to yourself! Be kind to yourself, accept that gift, and take to heart all the lessons you've learned so far in life. Go forward with the belief that you can make progress toward improving your life.

Your dream for a better life ignites the fire within. As you anticipate, develop, and work toward making it a reality, your life takes on renewed meaning and value... and starts getting better. You're taking charge, feeling more energetic, in control, on purpose, and excited... and others will want to associate with you.

When you do whatever it takes in working toward what matters to you, enjoying the journey as well as the results, your enthusiasm shines brilliantly, uplifting both yourself and others.

As your fire ignites it can spark others into action—it's contagious—and you start feeling even more optimistic and fired up. It's an upward spiral; and as you grow you'll find yourself more capable of bringing more aspirations to fruition.

We've all had fired up experiences, or have seen others fired up. Perhaps you saw the movie *The Son of God*. It was produced by the husband and wife team of Roma Downey and Mark Barnett (producer of TV's "Survivor" series) for $22 million. Developed out of their History Channel mini-series, *The Bible*, which broke all cable-TV records, was viewed by over 100,000,000 people!

In an interview shortly after the movie's release, the couple said producing the film not only deepened their faith, but also their friendship and marriage. They improved their own lives, while making a difference in the lives of countless others—wonderful benefits of following their dream.

This is but one example of a couple who got fired up and did whatever it took to achieve their dreams. As you work toward yours and become more fired up about them; you, too, can have a richer life experience.

Why Aren't More People Fired Up for a Better Life?

If it's true that we all have a fire inside, as well as unique gifts and talents, why aren't more people striving to improve their life situation? Part of the answer can be found due to the lack of participating in a proactive continuing educational, motivational, training program, along with being mentored, led, or coached for success, all in conjunction with a life-enriching opportunity or vehicle with which to make it happen. In addition, many who do or did have access to such a program and opportunity simply aren't or haven't availed themselves of it or aren't applying themselves in taking full advantage of what it has to offer, including the environment to move ahead personally and professionally.

Fortunately, examples of such programs can be found in popular fields like direct selling, relationship or referral marketing, personal selling, social or person-to-person commerce, and social sharing or selling, virtually all of which are home businesses. Then, too, franchise businesses have their own training and development programs to maximize the franchisees' success.

In the mid-1970s when I was teaching English and history to junior high students, I saw many youngsters negatively labeled by being placed in classes according to their "intelligence." While teaching a class of "low-level academic" ninth grade boys, I saw first-hand how destructive such labels are. Those boys didn't believe in themselves, considering themselves failures.

Speaking to them the first day, I did my best to "wipe their mental slates clean." I told them that every one of them could make an A—*if they worked for it.* At first, most of them didn't trust me. But as we spent more time together, they understood that I really did believe in them and wanted to help them learn.

Little by little, small miracles began to happen. One boy, who hated reading, began volunteering to read aloud to the class. Two others immediately saw their work pay off in the form of Bs on the first test. They were stunned! By the end of the year, there were many Bs, several Cs and only one D.

No one failed that class. And besides discovering they could read, write, and communicate effectively, these boys learned they were intelligent and capable, even though labeled otherwise. They had believed their label and their behavior reflected it. They needed someone to encourage them to achieve, just as we all do.

Negative labeling also happens to far too many adults. Sometimes they allow negative self-talk and childhood experiences to stop them from growing. They may have had harmful experiences where they were labeled as failures by others and, as a result, gave up on themselves. Unfortunately, schools aren't known to teach kids how to get and stay fired up and do whatever it takes to persistently work toward the kind of life they'd like to live.

That's exactly what this book is all about—a step-by-step handbook for defining what a better life means to you, and becoming and staying enthusiastic as you move forward in achieving it, while empowering others to do the same. These ideas have been used effectively by countless others to achieve their aspirations, and you can do the same. The encouraging stories included, like the following, are to reinforce the belief that you, too, can get fired up and improve your life in whatever manner you may choose.

Following Their Vision with Passion, These Two Fired Up People Helped Millions of Lives Improve

After setting the automotive world ablaze with his perfecting the assembly line, Henry Ford got fired up with the vision of also mass producing a V-8 engine cast as a single block, which had never been done before. Repeatedly told that it was impossible, he was nonetheless committed to it. Knowing his new vision was achievable; he sent his engineers back to work, telling them to stay on the job until they perfected the process.

A year later, the engineers reported that they still weren't successful. So, Henry told them to keep at it, *knowing* his determination, and their efforts, would pay off. Eventually, his engineers came through, and the Ford V-8 became a huge success. This was key in helping Henry Ford and his motor company outstrip the competition, taking the lead in the automotive marketplace. Ever the fired-up visionary, he refused to believe in "It's impossible."

Blessed Mother Teresa, one of the world's most beloved and admired people, was another person fired up with a magnificent vision. And even though she's no longer with us, her mission continues to flourish throughout the world, and she is still greatly revered.

At age 12, she started dreaming of being a missionary of love, and by 18, left her parent's home in Macedonia and studied to become a nun. In 1931, at the age of 21, she began teaching high school in Calcutta, and did so until 1948—when the suffering and poverty outside the convent walls inspired her to help the poorest of the poor.

Without any money, she followed her vision by humbly starting an open-air school for children of the slums. Her dedicated do-whatever-it-takes efforts soon began attracting others who believed in and wanted to participate in what she was doing, eventually forming a world-wide network. Her commitment also attracted the funding needed to make her vision a reality.

In 1950, after the Pope rejected her idea, she continued to persist until, incredibly, he finally gave her permission to start a new order, the Missionaries of Charity, with the primary mission of loving and caring for the unwanted. Along the way in expanding her outreach in helping others, she received numerous awards for her accomplishments, including the 1979 Nobel Peace Prize.

Today, her order includes over 4,000 nuns from 80 nationalities, and a million workers in more than 133 countries on five continents. By doggedly pursuing her dream, which she considered her duty, Blessed Mother Teresa has helped innumerable numbers of poor people, making a beautiful difference in the world... and her legacy continues doing so. This fired-up woman of small stature with a BIG dream, obviously lived her purpose, as challenging as it was, finding happiness in the process. As she said, *"Happiness is the natural fruit of duty."*

How It Feels to Be Fired Up for a Dream

Don Shula, famous six-time Super Bowl head football coach, and author, described what it felt like for him to be fired up. He wrote, "You want to know what motivates me? When the stadium's full, the crowd is yelling, and the referee raises his hand to signal the start of the game, I can feel the adrenaline rush through my body. I wouldn't want to be anywhere else in the world."

That attitude led Don to break George Hala's all-time coaching record of 324 wins with his 347, the most in NFL history. It spilled over into his owning a hotel and restaurants, and founding The Don Shula Foundation for Breast Cancer Research after his first wife passed away from the disease. He received the Ellis Island Medal of Honor in recognition of his humanitarian efforts.

Bonnie Blair, Olympic speed skater and five-time gold medalist, is a great example of someone completely fired up about her life and her dream. Every time she was interviewed on TV during the Olympics, she enthusiastically exclaimed, "I love to skate!"

There's nothing quite like the energy and excitement of being fired up. I actively strive to live more and more of my life fired up and, as a result, it doesn't take much to make it happen. One heartfelt talk with someone can spark my enthusiasm.

I also get excited when I picture myself helping others achieve their dreams. Remembering the times when I triumphed over obstacles to reach a special goal fills my heart with courage and the strength to keep going.

Do whatever it takes to get fired up. If the flame inside of you is not yet ignited, light it now. Light your fire today. The fired up attitude alone will help you to start living a better life. It'll also assist you in increasing your hope and bolstering your belief that you can strive for and achieve more of what you want.

Chapter 2
Negative Self-Talk Can
Douse Your Fire
Be Vigilant in Keeping Your Fire Alive

*"The inner speech, your thoughts, can cause you to
be rich or poor, loved or unloved, happy or unhappy,
attractive or unattractive, powerful or weak ."*
Ralph Charell

Negative self-talk is a liar and a thief. Did you know that we have 40-50,000 thoughts a day? Alarmingly, research has also shown that 75-to-85 percent of them are negative in most people. That's why being aware of and shutting down negative self-talk is so vital to success.

Two reasons why more people aren't living the lives they want are that they allow negative self-talk and limiting beliefs to stop them from taking appropriate action. Here are some examples of people who let negative self-talk run their lives, ruining their chances for success.

Rachael Lets Negativity Rule

Rachael sees an ad in a local online newspaper for the job she's always wanted. Instead of going after it and sharing her dynamism and excellent work skills with the people at that company, though, she doesn't even bother applying. Why? Even though she has the work experience, she thinks the lack of a degree will disqualify her. She undermines herself with negative self-talk and quits before she starts. She discouraged herself and gave up on her dream job.

Joe's Misperceptions Get in the Way of His Success

Joe reads a story about a local community center that needs volunteers to work with troubled youths. He's excited because he remembers how much an older man helped him when he was a struggling adolescent. But before he even meets anyone at the center, he lets his negative self-talk take over.

Perceiving that he doesn't have enough training in child psychology, he fears he won't know how to handle all the situations he'd encounter. He also thinks he needs to be earning lots of money to be a good role model. Then his wife tells him those kids might be dangerous, and he considers that possibility. The result is that he doesn't take action, allowing his doubts and fears to keep him stuck. He ends up feeling empty, miserable, and unfulfilled.

Jack and Susie's Negative Self-Talk Keeps Them Stuck

Jack and Susie's life is one of everyday mundane survival, barely getting by. Fortunately, a good friend, Harry, approached them with an opportunity to generate some additional income. This included the chance to take advantage of a system of continuing education so they could grow themselves personally and professionally, and create the better life they told him they wanted.

Even though Jack and Susie knew they were in a rut and unhappy with the way things were, they continued to let their fear of the unknown stop them, covering it up by giving Harry the excuse that they wouldn't have time for anything like that. The couple refused to take their friend up on his offer to help them change their circumstances, only to remain frustrated, bored, and broke. They didn't seem to understand the axiom..."*Insanity is doing the same thing over and over again, while expecting a different result!*"

Just in these three examples, it's evident how strong a hold negativity can have. Even though these people have let their false beliefs stop them, that doesn't mean you have to let yours stop you. With your enthusiasm, passion, talents, and willingness to go forward, you can improve your life.

Right now, you can start making changes in your life and begin doing whatever it takes to improve your life. You'll find that what you really want to accomplish reflects your innermost desires. Once you know that, you can start evaluating where you are and where you want to be. You'll start getting more and more fired up.

As you take steps toward improving your life, you'll start to discover that as long as you don't quit you could possibly give up the grind of working in an occupation or environment you no longer enjoy, while moving on in other exciting ways. Just be sure to have your financial situation in order before you do so.

The best way to make that happen is to take appropriate action and prepare yourself for your new life. Do your homework, lay the foundation, and "stack the deck" in your favor. Part of that is counseling with a leader, mentor, or success coach; someone you respect who has done what you want to do. Get fired up and do what it takes to make it a reality.

Perhaps these stories will remind you of someone you know. Later, you'll learn more about the doubts and fears that people allow to stop them from leading the kind of life they would like to live.

Everyone has a negative voice telling them they can't do it. Replace it with positive self-talk; tell yourself, "I can do it!" Then *take action,* no matter what the negative voice may say. Feel the fear, muster your courage, and go for what you want. When you make the decision and start taking action, wonderful things can happen in extraordinary ways. Here are a few examples:

Walt Disney

Going bankrupt several times before he succeeded, his dream kept him striving; he never quit. His cartoons, movies, and theme parks touch millions of lives every year. As Walt said...*"All of our dreams can come true [when] we have the courage to pursue them."*

Abraham Lincoln

He experienced many defeats before becoming one of the US's greatest presidents. Born poor, he lost his job, failed in business twice, and failed to get elected eight times before becoming a senator. He went bankrupt and later had a nervous breakdown. He never quit, persistently following his dream. What would the US be like if he had allowed his lack of formal childhood education and political failures stop him from running for president?

18

Michael Worsley

After he relocated to Manchester, New Hampshire, he discovered he was one of only a few black males in the area. Instead of dwelling on the isolation and developing a negative attitude, he put his skills to use. He channeled his energies into the Webster House, where he nurtured neglected children from broken homes, with self-esteem, love, and encouragement. He regularly received feedback from area professionals about the positive impact of his work on these children. He made a big difference in their lives, which, in turn, affected their behavior with others.

Is Fire and Enthusiasm Enough?

Success takes more than fire and enthusiasm—*it also requires commitment, determination, focus, planning, knowledge, personal and professional development, clarity, and consistent action.* It all starts with having a strong desire to make something happen.

Be clear about what you've been letting get in the way, and learn what you need to do to be more successful. The more information you have about what motivates you, the more you're enabled to keep going. The more you're aware of your false beliefs and negative self-talk, the easier it is to let them go and replace them with new beliefs and behaviors which support the achievement of your desires.

The more you use the ideas in this book while continually educating yourself about your career or business, the sooner you can improve your situation. Once you achieve your first objective you can use the same pattern of success over and over again to achieve others. You could also use this book to expand on your current aspirations, and work toward doing more of what you enjoy.

I'm Fired Up for a Better Life, Principle No. 1—Choose and Commit to Success

Do you realize how powerful choice and commitment are? Every great achievement came as a result of those two. Olympic athletes *choose* to spend hours and hours every day training for an event that comes only once every four years. After they have made the choice and committed to it, their actions and attitudes become their new normal.

When you make the choice to personally and professionally develop yourself and commit to it, you're saying yes to your future. You're actively setting into motion the *willingness* to succeed and the openness to opportunity and good fortune. You're instilling in yourself the attitude of doing whatever it takes. You're freeing up your thinking to help you achieve your desires. Such choice and commitment are deliberate and intentional; they clarify your direction and help you stay focused as you take action. As someone wise wrote…

"To win or lose,
To love or hate,
To strive or quit,
To risk or withdraw,
To accelerate or hesitate,
To dream or stagnate,
To open or close,
To succeed or fail,
To live or die.
Every one of these
Starts with a CHOICE."

So What's Your Choice?

The choice is yours. You can live the same life you've always lived—which may be just fine. But you're probably reading this book because you want your life to get better. Deep down inside, you may feel that your life is lacking in certain ways.

Perhaps it's not having enough time with your family, not being able to get out of debt, not making enough income, or not living in a big enough home. Maybe you're not satisfied with your current job or occupation, don't have enough time or money to relax, have fun, or travel as much as you'd like.

You might also want to touch the lives of others in a more positive way, contribute more to charity, live with more happiness and joy, and have more positive friendships, or perhaps something else. Whatever you desire, being fired up will help you make it happen.

To begin, simply *choose, commit,* and start *taking action.* Again, follow your dream and it'll take you where you're meant to go. Once you know the *why,* you'll figure out the *how* along the way. It only takes a tiny spark to light a huge fire; and you have countless sparks inside you. Start releasing them now to get yourself fired up and moving in the direction you want to go.

Chapter 3

What Do You Really Want?
Discovering the Spark Inside

"People are always blaming their circumstances...
I don't believe in circumstances. The people who get on in
this world... get up and look for the circumstances they
want, and if they can't find them, make them."
George Bernard Shaw

Where do you begin? Have you ever known anyone with enthusiasm and a sincere desire for a change, but they didn't know where to begin or even what they really want? This is quite common. Many have little or no idea how to think beyond their circumstances to discover it. They don't know how to make their rough ideas take shape and develop them into something they're excited about.

While many people have interest and curiosity, most need to get clearer about and be more committed to what they really want. So where do you start? It's really quite simple. Start thinking about what you'd enjoy doing most, or would like to accomplish or have, that you may have been wanting for some time. Dig deep.

I'm Fired Up for a Better Life, Principle No. 2—Dream-Build Often

Those who are the happiest, consistently successful, and fired up about their lives, always keep their dream for a better life in front of them. They make it a reality by regularly focusing on it and consistently taking action toward making it happen. They test drive the vehicle they'd like to own, and walk through homes they admire. They take pictures, bring brochures home, and look at them often.

Constantly stay in touch with heartfelt desires, both for yourself and your family, so you know why you're going the extra mile in building your business or profession. And be sure to take your spouse and children dream-building with you to keep them fired up for them too so they know what's in it for them to help you.

Greg Enjoys Giving Presentations and Sharing His Products, Services, and Opportunity with Others

Greg works from home, building his own business. Watching him in action when he meets with prospects, associates, and clients is exciting. He's fired up because he knows he's sharing something of value with people. The caring attitude he has for people shows in the way he listens and asks questions.

His excitement about what he's doing is obvious. His eyes light up, realizing he can help people with great products and services, and offer them the opportunity to overcome obstacles, grow, increase their income, and work toward bettering their lives. It's clear that he enjoys caring about, working with, and helping people. He's fired up when he shares what he has to offer with others, as he builds his future.

Sharing and Listening Can Build Dreams

The best way to understand something is to experience it. To know the feeling of being fired up that comes from talking about what you enjoy doing, do this next brief activity. It'll also give you the opportunity to practice effective listening. It only takes six minutes and it's a lot of fun. All you'll need is somebody who can sit with you for a few minutes, plus a stopwatch, clock, or timer. Pick someone who's supportive of you and what you're doing.

Set the timer for three minutes. Sit down and take turns playing the roles of sharer and listener. The sharer talks for three minutes about what he or she enjoys doing, going into detail about each activity, describing specifically what he or she loves about it; and keeps talking until the time is up.

If there are periods of silence, that's fine. The role of the listener is to actively listen; that means giving full attention to the sharer, not saying a word, just listening during those three minutes, even if there's silence. The listener is to have consistent eye contact with the sharer—giving full attention to that person, observing the level of enthusiasm and the twinkle in his or her eyes.

Speaker and author Bill McGrane III says, "Only when you listen...can you truly hear what the other person is saying...listening is loving. Give them your undivided attention. Listening requires more concentration than talking; it's the only way you can learn more about the other person." To be truly listened to is rare; a gift of great value. Give it generously.

After three minutes, switch roles and reset the timer. Now the first person listens attentively, silently, with total eye contact, while the "partner" shares about what *he or she* loves to do. The listener observes the body language to see how animated the partner becomes, and looks into their eyes for the sparkle. It's often a happy experience with a lot of laughter on both sides.

After both of you have shared, talk briefly about what you've experienced. Notice how you feel and what your voice sounds like. Most people become highly energized during this process, and use their hands as they talk faster, smile more, and even laugh. It's fun hearing others share what they love to do. It's also exciting sharing what you love doing which, as a bonus, serves you. Hearing yourself talk about it reaffirms your objective.

It's invigorating just anticipating doing more of what you enjoy. To earn that reward, persist toward your dream of living a better life by empowering and helping others to do the same, sometimes doing certain things you don't like or haven't yet learned how to do. Just keep going and growing until it all comes together, and you'll want to go and grow even more.

Choose to be fired up about life and all that it could hold in store for you. When you're wholeheartedly pursuing the betterment of your life, you're maximizing your ability to succeed and be happy. You're in the best state of mind possible to achieve your goals. You're excited, and that re-energizes you to make it happen.

I'm Fired Up for a Better Life, Principle No. 3—Pursuing a Better Life Makes a Difference in the World Around You

When you're working toward improving your life, you're automatically making a difference. Your fired-up attitude, happy joyful countenance, and enthusiasm can attract and inspire others to join and emulate you. It's like striking a match to dry kindling. Once the fire catches, one piece of kindling sparks and ignites the next, and then the next, and then the next, until a blaze is burning brightly.

The above listening activity can help you better understand yourself and others. It can assist you in fine-tuning your listening and observing skills.

The most effective leaders know that the best way to create long-lasting relationships is to *be sincerely interested in others*. Discover what would be part and parcel of their better life, and hark back to these dream elements as appropriate. This could include doing something as simple as sharing a travel video of their cherished vacation spot or activity, perhaps even watching it together. Or it may mean going through some beautiful homes nearby that are open to the public.

Eventually, the new people you're meeting will get it that you honestly care about them, and start relating with you as they enjoy being around you. As a result, they're likely to start considering you a friend. This can help your new relationships grow stronger and more positive, and these people are likely to be more receptive to what you have to share with them. They're more apt to understand that you have their best interests at heart.

Do Your Family and Friends Really Know You and Vice Versa?

Encourage family members, especially your spouse, to share what they love to do, so you can all be supportive of one another. Do you believe your family really knows what you enjoy doing?

If your family is among the small number who do freely share what they're most passionate about, consider yourself fortunate. Oftentimes, your relatives remember you as a child. Many of them may not realize how you've grown, what sparks your enthusiasm, how much you want to succeed, and what you're capable of doing.

How many unsuitable birthday presents have you received from family members and friends who you thought knew you? Do you want to develop stronger bonds with those you care about most? Find out what gets them fired up. Learn about their fondest desires, what they'd love to do or accomplish, where they'd like to go, and what they'd like to have. Make a point of asking about these things frequently, whether or not you share their interests.

Your attention will show that what matters to them, matters to you. It'll help you be a better spouse, parent, sibling, son, daughter, relative, or friend. This will also make it easier for you to share ideas and opportunities with them, if and when you choose to do so. Besides, it's great practice for relationship-building.

Your Fire for a Better Life Energizes Others

Did you know that other people can sense something different about you when you're diligently working toward bettering your life? It's true. You probably have a spring in your step and a sparkle in your eyes. Just like when you share what's on your heart to do and accomplish, your enthusiasm for life radiates to others.

One of the people at my bank often comments that I always sound so upbeat and positive when I talk to him on the phone. That's because I'm always working toward improving my life, while helping others improve theirs. I look forward to getting up in the morning and moving on. I'm fired up!

Can you imagine what the world would be like if more people would focus on bettering their lives, and help others do the same? The US statistics from Gallup polls say that nearly two-thirds of all people hate getting up and going to work. More heart attacks occur on Monday mornings before 9 a.m. than any other time.

What if these people were focused and working on improving their lives? What if they were energetic and excited about getting out of bed and starting their day? This, for sure, would be a different world, and certainly most amazing. The great thing is you can start creating the life you want right now, as you begin learning about what you want most out of it.

I'm Fired Up for a Better Life, Principle No. 4—Get Absolutely Clear About What You Really, Really Want

You must know what you want before you can focus on it, and you probably won't know that until you determine what constitutes your vision for a better life. Until you know that with absolute certainty you won't put your best efforts into it, and it'll take you much longer, if ever, to bring it to fruition.

Here's an activity to help you clarify that vision. Make two columns like those shown below. Number each item from one to ten. On the left, list ten things you have in your life right now which you don't want—*your circumstances.* On the right, opposite your circumstances, write down what you do want—*your desires.*

Circumstances or Desires—*What Controls Your Life?*

Circumstances	Desires
1. Debt/Overdue Bills	1. Financial security
2. A troublesome vehicle	2. A new vehicle
3. A boring job	3. Your own business
4. Too small a house	4. A big enough house

Draw an "X" through all circumstances. Before focusing on and putting energy into achieving your desires, know, for sure, what you want. You get what you focus on... provided you take consistent appropriate action until you achieve it.

For every desire, ask yourself: "If I could have this NOW, would I really want it; am I emotionally ready for it?" If the answer is anything but an absolute yes, cross it off. Put your attention on what you're *sure* you want. Clarity is key. You've got to have a true desire first before you start putting in the required effort that can make it a reality.

I personally know how well making this list works, after having done it years ago. When I was single, one desire on my list had been "a beautiful sunny home on the water" which, at that time, I had pictured as an oceanfront villa. Quietly sitting at home one evening, I got inspired by the idea of buying a new house. I checked the Sunday paper, and sure enough, there was an ad with a headline that read "Live on the Water." The advertised price told me I was financially ready to consider it.

I spent the entire afternoon walking around the property, which sat on a riverbank. It was easy to imagine living there—it was so lovely and peaceful. The very next day, I bought the property and soon began building the home I had envisioned, visiting the construction site every week, watching it take shape. Before too long, I was living in that beautiful sun-drenched home on the water.

You, too, can live in the home *you* want. Get fired up today and start doing whatever it takes to work toward creating your better life. Consider the words of Thomas Edison who got fired up by living his better life of being an inventor..."*I never worked a day in my life...it was all fun!*"

Chapter 4

What Are Your Favorite Activities?
Stir the Inner Sparks to Stay Fired Up

"Dreams put to work create the miracle."
Jim Rohn

One of the best ways to learn more about yourself and your desire for a better life is to consider what you'd love to do or do more of. You may be surprised at what you discover about yourself by taking a few minutes to list your favorite activities, how often you'd like to do them, and perhaps who'd you'd like to do them with. Also list any new activities you believe you'd like to participate in.

Some people learn that what they'd love to do doesn't cost much or is even free. Others realize it's been far too long a time since they've done some or any of those enjoyable activities. This is often because they haven't yet earned the personal freedom to do so, which to them would be part and parcel of their better life.

Others gain a greater realization of how important, or even precious, certain people are to them, causing them to want to improve those key relationships and spend more time doing their favorite things with those people. They then go on to actively develop their skills in becoming better spouses, parents, sons or daughters, and friends, as well as more effective and caring leaders, co-workers, and associates.

The happiest and most successful people stay in touch with and pursue what they love to do, and who they want to do it with.

27

They live fired up, letting their enthusiasm shine through in all areas of their lives. They've acknowledged their aspirations and are doing whatever it takes to grow, personally and professionally, so they can accomplish them.

They no longer make excuses why they "can't" do something. Instead, they look for reasons why they *can*. They know that consistently taking action will keep them fired up, and they *delay gratification* on activities and purchases that would interfere with making progress toward their objective of improving their lives. They've discovered, as bestselling author Dr. M. Scott Peck said…

"Delaying gratification is a process of scheduling the pain and pleasure of life…to enhance the pleasure…by meeting and experiencing the pain first and getting it over with. It's the only decent way to live."

Your Favorite Activities and Desired New Ones

Would you like to learn more about yourself and your desires? If so, list 15 favorite things you enjoy doing for fun, along with any new activities you'd like to do. Allow yourself to randomly list some ideas. If you come up with more than 15, that's great. Here's an example of how to set it up a grid:

My Favorite Activities

Activity	Last Done	Do with Others/Alone
1. Golf		
2. Read		
3. Learn and do new things		
4. Take my child to school		
5. Travel		
6. Eat at a nice restaurant		

Once you've made your list, review it and ask yourself two questions: When did you last do this activity? And, do you need or want certain special people in order to do it? Write down your answers next to the list. Consider whether these activities require advance planning, whether they support you mentally or physically, and whether they're structured or unstructured.

Like a good detective, take time to really learn about yourself and study your personal preferences. All of this information is quite useful when determining your objectives. Identifying your favorite activities gives significant clues about what you find meaningful and enjoyable.

Learning More About Yourself

As you review your list, you'll probably see a pattern. If the things you love to do often require little or no planning, you're probably a spontaneous, fun-loving person. If most of your favorite activities require advance planning or structure, you probably prefer a more organized lifestyle. You're less likely to do things spontaneously and more likely to plan your life.

If physical risk is involved in most of your favorite activities, you probably prefer excitement over security, freedom over structure, creativity over analysis. If most of your favorite activities are about your physical health, that's a key priority for you and something you value highly. Many of your life choices will be based on whether something is good for you physically. Keeping fit is probably a primary goal in your life.

Study this list and you may learn things about yourself which you might not have thought much about before. Your favorite activities provide valuable clues about what gets you fired up. They say a great deal about your personality and values. Later, we'll discuss how they fit with your life purpose.

One question to ask yourself when you look at your list is: *How long has it been since I did the things I love?* When you do things that get you fired up, you're happy and have a cheerful attitude. If you haven't done any of your favorite things for a while, you may want to treat yourself by doing so as a reward for achieving a goal.

Imagine how good you'll feel when you're fired up, working toward setting yourself up so you can do more of what you want to do. Picture how pleasant it'll be when you can spend more time doing the things that interest and excite you, with the people you care about and enjoy most.

Blend What You Love to Do with Your Business or Profession

Given your priorities, a great way to get the most out of your investment in building your business or profession is to mix business with pleasure as often as may be appropriate. Whenever there's a business event out of town, you could use any free time you may have to see the local attractions. Or, if you can easily afford to do so, you could get there a day early or stay a day longer. You'll be investing in your future, while enjoying the present. Be sure to check your financial situation and business schedule before you make any plans.

Chapter 5

Use Your Imagination to
Fire Up Your Desire for a Better Life
Stoke the Fire Inside

*"If one advances confidently in the direction of his
dreams, and endeavors to live the life he has imagined, he
will meet with a success unexpected in common hours."*
Henry David Thoreau

The fire of life is inside you and, because of it, you *can* live the life you've always wanted. Since you've gotten this far, it's likely you really do want to improve your life situation. But maybe you still don't have enough clarity about it. Read on and you'll find more ways to help you discover what you really want out of life, then you can move toward making it a reality.

To help with this, you'll learn about other people like you who did whatever was necessary to improve their lives. Your discovery process can be easy and fun, and you'll be amazed at how much progress you can make in a short time. So let yourself enjoy the adventure; it's all for you. Just imagine...

I'm Fired Up for a Better Life, Principle No. 5—Use Your Imagination

Your imagination is a powerful tool that can help you resolve tough situations and fuel your aspirations. Famous Olympic athletes the world over have mentally pictured their success for decades. One study showed that the German and Russian Olympic athletes spent 75 percent of their training time envisioning their peak performance. That meant they were doing the actual physical training only 25 percent of the time. Today, many professional athletes regularly focus on and imagine their victories; they mentally see themselves winning. Picturing their success helps them make it a reality.

Former Decathlon Champion Dan O'Brien practiced every day for years to go to the Olympics. Four years prior to his achievement he had faced the heartbreak of not qualifying at the trials, but Dan was determined not to let that happen again. At home, he jogged every day, picturing himself running victoriously through the Olympic stadium.

Dan imagined himself wearing the gold medal and the crowd calling out his name over and over as he was presented with the title, "The world's greatest athlete." He called himself that every day, affirming it as *the truth in advance*. With the heart and mind of an Olympian, Dan got fired up for the next Olympics. He realized his objective when he won the Decathlon Gold, reclaiming it for the US—for the first time in 20 years!

The Clearer You Are the More You're Likely to Make It Happen

It's essential to clearly define what you really want in vivid detail. However, if you're still fuzzy about it or it's even a complete mystery, take heart. You're going to have a chance right now to gain more clarity about your sincere desires.

One of the best ways to gain more information is to *imagine* each of your desires fully realized in all its glory. Thomas Edison spent a great deal of time imagining how he wanted his life to be. To stay refreshed and creative so his imagination could run free, he often took naps and encouraged his employees to do the same.

In fact, Edison got some of his best ideas while daydreaming, focusing on what he wanted to do. That's why it's smart for you to do this as well. It'll help you access the creative part of your brain and gain valuable insight as to how your life could be. It'll help you get fired up.

Picture What You Really Want—Daydream

Take a few minutes now to relax and picture what you really want. See yourself debt free and having the income and savings you'd really like to have. Picture yourself enjoying more time with family and friends. Imagine taking wonderful vacations, going places you've always wanted to go, doing what you've always wanted to do.

Picture yourself living in the home you want, with the mortgage paid off, and being able to hire a cleaning person and someone to do lawn and garden work if you so desire. Imagine having the personal freedom to come and as you please, knowing your home's maintenance has been delegated.

Now imagine yourself being fired up at a convention, being recognized on stage for having reached a new level in your business or profession. Sense how terrific you feel, how thankful, how successful, how happy. You've been focusing on your goals and you're seeing them come to fruition.

As you move on, you may travel and share your story at seminars. You'll inspire others and see them enthusiastically respond to your excitement, sincerity, and winning track record.

Notice how people follow your example and seek your guidance and wisdom. Listen to their comments and questions and give them your best. Watch yourself empowering and helping them move on, making a difference in their lives. You're becoming a great leader. As former US President John Quincy Adams said... *"If your actions inspire others to dream more, learn more, do more, and become more you are a leader."*

Observe how your life has changed for the better. How are you spending your time? Where are you living and who are you surrounding yourself with? Notice how much more fulfilling your life has become and how healthy and energized you feel.

How does it feel to be financially secure and doing more of what you love to do? What are others saying to you? What are you saying to others? Listen to the happiness and commitment in your voice; feel your passion and sense of purpose. You know your contribution is valuable, particularly for your family, friends, close associates, and others.

What does your life look like? What's happening? How and where are you doing your business or profession and enjoying your life? They seem like one and the same, don't they? You're delighting in it so much; it's hard to believe that this is how you've earned your better life. What does the world look like to you from this perspective? See it clearly. Feel your deep sense of satisfaction and gratitude.

Take your time and experience only good things; see all the positive aspects of your life as it unfolds in your mind... and feel your own excitement and vitality. Allow your creative imagination to paint a vivid picture; make it real with sounds and smells and colors. Observe the people and feel the emotions. Let your imagination get you fired up. See it all in a positive way as totally fulfilling—and be thankful for it.

Start Exploring, Trusting What You Discover

After daydreaming for several minutes, make some notes about your experience by writing or just talking into a recorder. Did you know that whatever you say into a recorder, you also "load" into your subconscious? Wouldn't it be powerful to load your description of your vision of the life you want and its resulting feelings of greater happiness and joy into your internal "audios"? Perhaps you found yourself imagining doing something you never even considered before, and you got a new vision, which often happens during this activity.

Note your feelings, actions, family, friends, and lifestyle, even if some of it seems unfamiliar to you now. All of this is important information as you gain greater clarity about igniting your internal fire. You may not understand the exact nature of what you were doing; but it just felt right. That's perfectly normal. You probably have more wisdom about your deepest desires than you may have thought. All it takes is the courage to... *start exploring, trusting what you discover.*

One couple who did this got such clear ideas about the life they longed for (which was very different from their situation at the time) that they changed their lives considerably in six months. Envisioning themselves financially secure with more time for family and friends, they got moving, earnestly starting to build their own business, while maintaining their jobs.

As their business grew, they found their personal and professional lives improving. After a while, they were being recognized for their accomplishments and traveling to prime vacation spots.

They didn't realize what their life was supposed to really be all about until they started striving to better it. Prior to that, they had been in the daily grind, not really thinking about how their life could be, taking it for granted just like most of the people they knew. The turning point came when they went forward in faith believing in and imagining their new life as clearly as they could picture it.

Now congratulate yourself on your progress so far. Acknowledge yourself for doing these activities and putting positive energy into your life. You're worth it! Enjoy this pleasant process; savor it like your favorite meal. Let it sink in, grow richer, and become more and more real to you.

It's still too new to expose to possible critics, so don't share it with anyone you think might try to "burst your bubble." Let it blossom under your tender loving care. Since one thing leads to another, you'll undoubtedly get more ideas and greater clarity as you go along. You're opening up the floodgates to a better life.

Sometimes when you're resting in bed, you may come up with more ideas about what you'd like to have in your new life. Be sure to keep your mobile device or notebook by the bed for just that reason, and write down your ideas. And again, share your vision only with those closest to you who you believe would be supportive. These could be people like your spouse, success coach, leader, or mentor.

Remind yourself of all the successes you've had in your life so far. You have unique gifts and talents to share with others. Remember, *you were born to win.* Let that get you fired up. Pat yourself on the back for your progress and your new awareness of yourself and what you truly want in living a better life. You're starting to take action and move on. Bravo!

Chapter 6

Have Any Myths About Success?
Step Outside Your Comfort Zone to Get Fired Up

*"Being unready and ill-equipped is what you have to
expect in life. It's the universal predicament—circumstances
are seldom right. You must do with less than you need."*
Charlton Ogburn, Jr.

Why do some people truly succeed, while most don't?
One of the greatest culprits is *doubt*. People who
allow the limiting beliefs they learned during childhood, or even later on, to stop them are highly
unlikely to even try to improve their lives in any meaningful way.

False beliefs, myths, or delusions are the success-stealers that,
if not recognized for what they are, keep people from stretching
outside their comfort or familiar zones, and going for the success
they'd really like to have. If they stay in those zones they can't
grow and succeed. But if they intend to succeed, they must grow,
causing themselves to be uncomfortable to whatever degree, which
is the way of success. If they insist on hanging on to their myths,
even after knowing what they are, they're sabotaging their own
potential for success, happiness, and a more meaningful life.

***I'm Fired Up for a Better Life*, Principle No. 6—*Uncover Your
Myths About Success***

People often learn myths as kids or through unpleasant life experiences, which restrict their thinking and hold them back.

Sometimes parents, though well-intended, pass along an inappropriate statement like, "If you want to get ahead in this world, you have to know the right people."

A more helpful bit of advice is, "If you want to get ahead in this world, find a need and work diligently to fill it." Or, "If you want to get ahead in this world, make sure as many people as possible get to know you and what you have to offer, coupling that with an attitude of wanting to serve them well and doing so."

Your parents weren't intentionally setting up roadblocks. They probably believed they were motivating you with what they thought was true, which you probably believed without question. And since your subconscious can't evaluate, it just accepted it all.

Those who don't have someone or something exerting a positive influence in their lives—teaching them that *challenges are essential to learn, grow, and succeed*—develop myths that limit their belief in themselves and their abilities. Instead of viewing every obstacle as a necessary step in the process of succeeding, when they stumble they label themselves failures, believing they can't win. They have no one to encourage them over the hurdles.

During adolescence, they may have been taught or adopted, perhaps from their peers, other destructive myths like: "I'm not good enough," "I'll never have what I want," or "Nobody likes me or my ideas; I'm a reject." These myths can be destructive during youth, and rarely helpful in adulthood... *unless* the individual takes them as challenges to be overcome.

Sometimes myths become so deeply ingrained in the subconscious, that they become detrimental, even dangerous, to one's future. They can cause people to make excuses that destroy their possibilities for success, leading them to give up on themselves and their aspirations, maybe even causing them to be naysayers for others. Most people don't realize this is happening because it's become a habit—a self-defeating habit.

Discover what myths you're telling yourself and replace them with positive affirmations like, "I can do this!" to help you succeed. You'll be happier and healthier, as well. (We'll discuss affirmations later.) *Your awareness of your myths is key to letting them go.* You're likely to be amazed to learn what untruths may be dwelling in the depths of your subconscious. Take the time to investigate. Learn to laugh at your myths and release their negative hold on you. This can make all the difference in the world.

Here are three actions steps to help you learn more about your own false beliefs. Each one is short and fun, and can help you be more successful. Be sure to do all three.

Action Step 1A to Learn More About Your False Beliefs—*Talk with Your Leader, Mentor, or Success Coach,* someone who's understanding and supportive as well as a good listener. Many family members think they really know you, but it's all based on their limited perspective of you; they fail to see your potential.

Sit down with your leader, mentor, or success coach and just talk about your aspirations, and what you believe is stopping you from going for them right now, today, in this very moment. Record the myths that surface while you talk. Make a list of them. Continue sharing until you believe you've covered all the possible blocks to your success.

Action Step 1B to Learn More About Your False Beliefs—*Review Your Personal History.* Find a nice, quiet place where you won't be disturbed, and turn on some soft soothing music. It's likely you've already been successful in many areas of your life. But for now, look at your disappointments. Think back over your life and consider what you have yet to achieve. Pay attention to the limiting beliefs (myths) that may have held you back. Determine if you're still allowing them to have destructive "power" over you, or if you've moved on from their hold.

One way to do this is to say the myth out loud and notice whether you feel upset in your stomach or just uneasy. If so, you're still letting these beliefs have destructive power over you. If you just laugh or have no reaction, then your limiting belief no longer affects you. Make a written list of those you still find difficult to think about.

Action Step 1C to Learn More About Your False Beliefs—*Take the Success-Stealer Test.* Listed below are several common success-stealing thoughts. People often let them get in the way of their living better lives, without even realizing it, inadvertently using them as excuses not to do what it takes to be more successful. Read over the list and check mark those you believe are true. Realize which ones you've *allowed* to get in the way of your being more successful, and write down any others that may come to mind.

Every false belief in the list below begins with the words: People who want a better life must...

- Have a lot of money.
- Have a college degree.
- Be well-connected.
- Be selfish.
- Be healthy and fit.
- Have a lot of "free" time.
- Be 100 percent confident at all times.
- Be well-organized.
- Have tons of energy.
- Be gifted or talented.
- Be very intelligent.
- Be fearless.
- Risk everything.
- Be good-looking.
- Be young (or old).
- Have independent sources of income.
- Forget about time with their family.
- Be totally unique.
- Have everything perfect with no challenging people or circumstances in the way.
- Be of a certain race or ethnicity.
- Fill in the blank _____

Now that you've completed the action steps above, are you ready to laugh about your success-stealing beliefs? Do you now realize how untrue they are and that they really have no power over you and don't deserve to have a place in your mind?

Action Step 2—*Laugh a Little.* Henry Ward Beecher said...*"Mirth is God's best medicine."* Laughter can help you get a new perspective on the myths you've allowed, up until now, to get in the way of your living a better life. Look over your list and notice how silly some of these beliefs are. Some of them may even seem to contradict each other. Some make no sense at all, yet they remain myths in far too many people's minds.

Without exception, I can give you examples of real-life people who prove every one of these myths is false. So relax and laugh a little at the words. Soon they'll have no power over you because you will have let them go, eliminating their hold on you.

Action Step 3—*Let the Myths Go.* Whatever you learned by doing action Steps 1A through 1C, get a sheet of paper and write down the myths that you've allowed to affect you. Here are two of the many ways you can let them go:

A—For each myth you've written on the list write a positive statement in its place to invalidate it. For example:

MYTH—A college degree is required for a better life.

POSITIVE TRUE STATEMENT—People of any educational level can have better lives, provided they're in the right income vehicle and they do whatever it takes in working for it.

After you have done this for *each* myth, go to B.

B— Draw a big "X" through the list of myths.

If it gives you more satisfaction, individually cross out each myth. Next, tear up that piece of paper into tiny little pieces, while saying out loud, *"I permanently let go of these limiting beliefs. I am now free to live a better life."* If you like, you can also burn those pieces of paper, symbolically destroying the myths. While this may sound a bit silly, *it works!* It can be quite powerful. Feel the relief that comes when you are no longer carrying that emotional garbage. Let it all go, and get on with it.

I'm Fired Up for a Better Life, Principle No. 7—*Identify Role Models*

To succeed in life, we all need excellent role models—people who beat the odds and won. They show us that if they can make it, so can we. These people need not be big, famous heroes; it could be the child with a mental or physical challenge who finally got on the baseball team. Or it could be a local physically challenged person who's inspiring other people to overcome their obstacles. Or it may be the bus driver who has won safety and courtesy awards, who called you by your name every morning and said you could do anything you set your mind to.

Take a minute now to think about the inspirational role models in your life. Who are they? Are they well-known people in or out of your field of endeavor, or are they relatively unknown people like a close friend, your teacher, your mother or father, your grandmother or grandfather, or your next door neighbor?

What did they do for you? How did they touch your life? Oftentimes, you'll discover that it was all the little things they did for you throughout the years that made the difference, not necessarily something big.

When you're working toward improving your life, it helps to contact those people who inspire you. Tell them how they touched your life and thank them. Everyone, no matter how successful or famous, loves to hear sincere feedback about how they made a difference in the lives of others. When you share with them from the heart, chances are they'll encourage you even more.

From my early years on, my grandmother McClamroch was a tremendous role model for me. Her parents were killed in a car crash when she was 12, and she went to live with an aunt and uncle. Going through such tough times, emotionally and financially, taught her to be self-reliant. She went to Goucher College and later married a college professor from another university.

While her husband was in the US Army during World Wars I and II, she organized the local women, made bandages and kept things going at home. She beat several different kinds of cancer before she died in her mid-70s. Her courage and perseverance strongly influenced me. By her example, she empowered me to overcome my challenging childhood and keep moving toward my aspirations.

Talk with a Leader You Admire

"(Leader's Name), I just want you to know that I admire you for the way you've built your success and care about people. It's obvious you're a great leader, and I know that I could learn a lot from you. I'm serious about my future and will do whatever it takes to make it happen. Would you have time to mentor, coach, or guide me? I'd really appreciate it."

Another way you could start would be "(Name), your recent seminar really touched my heart. It's amazing how you've overcome so many obstacles to get where you are. You've really inspired me to learn how to better support and encourage others. Would you be in a position to counsel me and offer me some guidance? I really think you could help me and would very much appreciate your time. I will follow your advice."

Approaches like these are powerful and effective. Everyone who has succeeded has overcome many challenges. They can relate to your needs when you show them respect, courtesy, and sincere admiration. Always honor their time and stick to the main issues. Leaders always welcome those who are serious about bettering themselves and achieving more. You'll be delighted with how helpful they can be.

Leaders always feel honored and humbled when someone calls, emails, sends a card, or writes a note telling them how their lives were touched. If you're already a leader, you'll understand.

I'm Fired Up for a Better Life, Principle No. 8—Read Positive Books, Listen to Motivational/Educational Audios, and Attend Seminars

I've personally benefited greatly by *reading positive books*, and you can too. Ask your leader, mentor, or success coach to recommend some good books to you that will help you grow and become the best you can be, both personally and professionally.

Reading such books only 20 minutes a day can make a big difference and empower you to increase your success on the job, in business, and in life. Just one idea can set you on fire, and help you empower others in their desire to improve their lives.

Another way to stay fired up and moving forward is by *listening to motivational and educational audios* every day, as part of your continuing education. People who are really moving on make this a habit. Perhaps your company or organizational leader has or can recommend some audios you could take advantage of.

Audios are especially convenient because you can listen to them while getting ready for work or bed, taking a walk or run, or working around the house or yard. You could also make your vehicle(s) a "university on wheels." Turn off the negative news, load the audio, "play" it, and get fired up!

It's been said that to fully benefit from an audio, you need to listen to it 17 times, as we retain only about six percent of what we hear. So make it a habit to listen to audios on a daily basis.

Attending seminars can also help you stay fired up to overcome obstacles and keep going. Associating with other winners, can help you stay on track and accelerate your growth and momentum. I've been going to seminars for years, and have found that they really make a difference. Doing so has helped keep me motivated and empowered in making progress with my business.

Again, just one simple but profound idea heard on an audio or at a seminar, or read in a book, can enrich your life and get you fired up. The entire cost—really an investment in yourself (the greatest one you can make!) and, of course, your business—of regularly attending seminars, listening to audios, and reading books is of inestimable value. Once you've developed these three habits, you'll realize how much fun it is to stay fired up.

You never know when one idea will supercharge you with fired-up energy for a breakthrough, or just how infectious that idea could be for the fired-up-ness of those associated with you. Keep doing what it takes to get educated, inspired, empowered, and motivated.

Another benefit of seminars, audios, and books is having what you believe confirmed, clarified, or expanded upon by others, helping you realize you're not alone in your quest. For example, the speaker or author may share how they overcame an obstacle that you may be dealing with right now.

Associating with like-minded people—via audios, books, and online and on-site events—who have been or are on a similar path, perhaps with similar challenges, can inspire and empower you. The knowledge and energy gained from doing these activities can stoke everyone's fire to an extraordinary degree. As Ben Franklin said...

"An investment in knowledge pays the best interest."

I'm Fired Up for a Better Life, Principle No. 9—Act "As If"... with Enthusiasm

One of the best ways to ignite your sparks and get fired up is to act as if you've already accomplished what you want to do. First, make your desire come alive in your mind and heart, setting the stage for you to make it a reality. This is a key part of what being fired up is all about. Acting as if...with enthusiasm... is essential to the achievement process. Act as if your aspiration is already a part of your life.

For example, when I was building my house, I visited it every week, imagining what it would feel like to live there. Driving a vehicle you'd like to have or visiting or driving by home you'd love to live in can make your flames burn higher and brighter.

Even something as simple as *dressing the part,* from super casual to sporty or professional, of how you want to live can change the way you feel about yourself. Olympic Champion, super sprinter Florence Griffith Joyner, used clothes as a key tool for acting as if. Wearing brightly colored running outfits and beautifully painted fingernails, Florence went on to win three gold medals. She said of dressing the part...

"My outfits represent the belief, determination, discipline, and desire to make my dreams come true...."

Start acting as if your better life is a foregone conclusion, which it already has started to become because of your shift to a fired-up attitude. You can't make it happen with a wimpy, low-energy, lackluster attitude.

The more vividly you can see, hear, and feel yourself living your improved life, the more likely you are to fully realize it. This, in turn, will help you become more familiar with your desire, creating a stronger belief that you can do it. Since you've already integrated this new "experience" into your mind and heart, your desire then becomes your new comfort and familiar zone.

You start expecting it to happen in reality since it has already happened in your mind, which has to happen before any new idea can become a reality. As a result, it seems perfectly natural to do whatever it takes to go to your next level of success, which is realized by striving until you create the results you want.

Congratulations on your progress so far. You've made a great start by letting go of your myths. Work hard and smart and you could have whatever your heart desires. Keep moving!

Chapter 7
Vision, Mission, and Purpose
Laying the Foundational Logs of Your Fire

"All significant battles are waged within the self."
Sheldon Kopp

When does your better life actually begin? Again, as soon as you start getting fired up about what you want, your attitude—and therefore your life—begins to improve. It's an inside job.

So you may wonder, "How do I begin to further define what a better life is for me?" An excellent place to start is with your life vision, mission, and purpose.

Your vision, mission, and purpose all relate to your values and what you consider meaningful and important. In Dr. Martin Luther King's famous 1960s speech, "I Have a Dream," his purpose and mission were very clear. He envisioned a society where the United States would...

"...one day rise up and live out its creed...that all men are created equal...where my children will not be judged by the color of their skin, but rather by the content of their character," and *"...where black men and white men, Jews and Gentiles, Protestants and Catholics will be able to join hands and say 'free at last, free at last. Thank God Almighty, we are free at last.'"*

That got him fired up and led him to inspire millions of people, even to this day. Whenever I watch a video of him delivering that speech, I can feel his passion. He was an exceptional gentleman who lived and died for his principles.

Your life purpose can be a great driving force as well. It can help you break through any barriers that may have been in your mind or your environment. It can move you to rise above previous so-called limitations and do more than you ever thought possible.

Vision, Mission, and Purpose

Your *vision* is the loftiest expression of what you truly want for your life. It's your mental picture of hope and optimism of the ideal. You may be familiar with these powerful biblical words...

"Where there is no vision, the people perish."

A vision might relate, for example, to how a business owner would like his or her organization to be in the future. You might have a vision for your business or profession of spreading around the world, impacting people everywhere in a positive way.

A *mission statement* reflects what and how you contribute to the world. It's based on how you are implementing your life purpose, for example, through building your own business.

Your *life purpose* relates to what you are meant to do in your life, as you feel it in your heart.

Purpose is the core of both the mission and the vision which, for example, originates in the heart and soul of a business's founder. Perhaps he or she lost a parent to an illness that could have been treated with the right products, so the founder wants to offer products which can help save or enhance other people's lives. Or maybe the founder has a burning desire to excel and make a difference in an unusual way that will also have a large impact on how the business is conducted.

Living on purpose will make you feel good about yourself. You'll be serving others the best way you possibly can, in line with your desires... which are the keys to enhancing your gifts, talents, and abilities.

It's All About Values

Fundamental to vision, mission, and purpose are your core values—the qualities you consider the most significant that also exert a tremendous force on your life. They shape your attitudes, beliefs, and relationships. Know what you value most when planning for and anticipating your upgraded life. Start by including what's most important to you as reflected by your core values.

Which of These Core Values Apply to You?

1. *Financial Security*—having the money to handle your economic responsibilities; using it wisely and keeping yourself free from money-related difficulties.
2. *Safety*—having physical, emotional, or mental protection where you feel free from attack and danger.
3. *Freedom*—having the opportunity and independence to live the life you choose.
4. *Success*—the process of working toward the achievement of a worthwhile dream, goal, or objective; it's a journey.
5. *Joy*—feeling great delight or elation caused by something exceptionally good, satisfying, or meaningful; keen pleasure and euphoria.
6. *Love*—having healthy, caring relationships with family, friends, and associates, especially with that special person with whom you have a committed marital relationship.
7. *Good Health*—the state of being physically, emotionally, mentally, and spiritually sound.
8. *Personal Integrity*—conducting your life honestly at all times; believing in and doing the right things.
9. *Service*—helping and contributing to the lives of others.
10. *Peace of Mind*—feeling a sense of serenity and freedom from negative stress.
11. *Ease*—a sense of relaxation and comfort.
12. *Spirituality*—matters relating to belief in God; your faith.
13. *Creativity*—freely and fully expressing your gifts, talents, and abilities however you may choose.
14. *Personal Growth*—continually refining and developing your inner qualities and people skills, while learning from your mistakes and moving on. Working on improving yourself.
15. *Professional Growth*—committed to an ongoing program of learning more about your chosen field, while staying motivated and always striving for excellence, becoming better than your current best.
16. *Greatness*—making a significant impact on the world, sometimes leading to public recognition and awareness of what you're doing on a large scale.
17. *Humility*—being aware of your unskilled behavior, based on your understanding that no one succeeds alone; having no arrogance.

18. **Order**—dealing with your environment so everything is struc-
    tured and well-organized.
19. **Humor**—being able to laugh alone or with others, and not
    taking yourself too seriously.
20. **Talent**—the ability to learn or do a specific skill or art form.
    It can be either inherent or developed.

Values Activity

In addition to those above, add any other values that are important to you. Out of both of those lists, write down your top five in
their order of importance to you:

1._____   2._____

3._____   4._____

5._____

Now study this list. It'll provide you with a great deal of useful
information. Your top five values will shape your life decisions the
most, giving you the best clues about what really gets you fired up.

Discovering Your Life Purpose

Believe it or not, discovering your life purpose can be quite
easy when you break it down into a simple, clear statement. Be
aware that you may have more than one purpose, which you could
express in a variety of ways. To give you some ideas, here are
three possibilities, one of which may fit you:

1. To care about others by sharing fine products and services, as
    well as proven success principles via a worthy income op-
    portunity, all of which can help them live better lives.

2. To use profits from my business or profession to establish a
    foundation and home for underprivileged children.

3. To use profits from my business or profession to build a
    chain of restaurants to serve people healthy foods in an up-
    lifting environment.

The key is to be open and flexible. Imagine you're a private
detective investigating your own life. You gather as many clues

as possible, write them down, and mindfully and heartfully consider how to make sense of it all.

Taking it one step at a time, persist until you discover the truth during what could be a fascinating and profound experience. For many, it comes as a tremendous relief to know why they're alive here on this earth, and to deeply understand what's truly important to them.

Developing Your Life Purpose Statement

Here are four questions to help you develop your life purpose statement. Take about 30 minutes; if not convenient now, be sure to do it later. This is a very important process, not to be taken lightly. So do it only when you can invest sufficient time to focus on it and allow the information to really resonate with you and sink in.

You can discover your life purpose by knowing what you enjoy doing the most, what interests you most, what gets you fired up, and what qualities most represent you. All of this is clearly an expression of what you value. It's as simple as that.

Your Life Purpose Statement, Question No. 1—*What Are Your Two Best, Most Unique Qualities?* As you identify your particular qualities, start by making a list of what you believe to be all of your best traits. Then go back and underline the two you feel most uniquely represent you, and for which you'd most like to be known and remembered. If you're still not sure, ask a supportive family member or friend what they believe are your best and most unique qualities. These are often the qualities people frequently comment on, without which you would not be who you are.

For example: *A great leader, really cares about others, has a good sense of humor, and is flexible, humble, and teachable.*

Your Life Purpose Statement, Question No. 2—*How Do You Enjoy Expressing Those Two Most Representative Traits?* Now list your favorite ways of expressing those qualities; use verbs ending in "ing." Then pick your top two favorite forms of expression and underline them. When you express yourself in these two favorite ways, you feel happy and have a sense of positive well-being, delight, and freedom. If there's any resistance at all to a form of expression, then it's probably not your favorite way of sharing your two best and most unique qualities.

For example: _Sharing success ideas_, teaching, _empowering and helping others_, flying, skiing, running.

Your Life Purpose Statement, Question No. 3—_How Would You Describe Your Version of an Ideal World?_ Here you simply describe what your ideal world would be like, as if time, money, and circumstances were no object. This is a vision statement because it has hope, optimism, and an expression of the ideal in it.

Include what you believe are the most vital elements, underlining the top two. What would address world problems that most disturb you? What would ensure a positive world for the future? These are all to be _your_ choices and _your_ opinions. That's all that matters here. So it's best not to consult anyone else on this question, or you may be influenced by his or her ideas of what would be a perfect world for you.

For example: _It's a peaceful, healthy world where people engage in free enterprise and help others grow personally and professionally so they can live better lives_.

Congratulations! You're almost done. You know what makes you unique and you're more aware of your favorite ways for expressing your uniqueness. You've also defined your ideal world.

All of this information forms the foundation of your life purpose. Now look over the answers to the above three questions, and keep them in mind as you answer Question No. 4.

Your Life Purpose Statement, Question No. 4—_How Would You Summarize Your Life Purpose Statement Using Your Answers to the Three Questions Above?_ Combine all of the elements of the previous three questions into one single life purpose statement. One way to summarize your life purpose statement is to write "Using my," then add your two top qualities and follow with "I am...so that others may...."

For example: _Using my leadership abilities and caring about others, I'm sharing success ideas and empowering and helping them grow personally and professionally so they can live better lives._

Here Are Some Other Examples of Life Purpose Statements

They're all from ordinary people. They were not born with any special talents or gifts that could make them more likely to succeed than others. They're simply fired up about their life purpose.

- Ed, a national youth trainer, developed this life purpose statement: "As a loving, courageous, and compassionate man, I inspire the youth of today through fun and enthusiasm and have tremendous impact on their lives." His vision is a world of children who feel good about themselves and are confident, productive members of society. His mission is to teach youth leadership skills with excellence and enthusiasm.

- Will, an American working in Bulgaria, writes his life purpose statement: "Honestly and clearly sharing my life experiences and knowledge, I am creating and promoting world community and peace." His vision is a world which is one large community, with everyone respecting and appreciating each other's uniqueness. His mission is to bring business tools and techniques to budding entrepreneurs in underdeveloped parts of the world and assist them in becoming financially independent.

As you read these statements, it's obvious how distinct each one is. Everyone finds a unique way to express his or her purpose and live a more satisfying life—just like you're doing. As you grow and achieve various objectives, the expression of your purpose may change.

However, you can use your life purpose statement as a key reference point throughout your life, especially when you're making major decisions and planning each year. Your true happiness depends on living your life in tune with your life purpose.

You might want to share your life purpose statement with someone you trust who cares about you, like your spouse, leader, success coach, or mentor. You could print it out onto a small piece of paper and carry it in your wallet or purse, or enter it into your time/activity management system or mobile device. You could also tape it to your bathroom mirror to remind you why you're alive.

Whatever you choose to do, *honor it and yourself by doing it!* There's only one you. You're a rare individual with a treasured vision, mission, and purpose that only you can express.

"One can never consent to creep when one feels an impulse to soar. Your success and happiness lies in you. Resolve to keep happy, and your joy and you shall form an invincible host against difficulties. Optimism is the faith that leads to achievement. Nothing can be done without hope and confidence. Life is either a daring adventure or nothing at all."

Helen Keller

Chapter 8

Putting It All Together
Building on Your Fire's Foundation

"Man alone, of all creatures, can change his pattern, as he's the architect of his destiny. To change your life: Start immediately. Do it flamboyantly. No exceptions."
William James

Learn to embrace and appreciate everyone and everything that supports the process of working toward a better life, so you can do more of what you enjoy most. When you're building a career or business that can give you the life you'd like to live, you'll discover how beautifully your life purpose and favorite activities relate to each other.

When you're working toward and gradually living more of the life you long for and doing more of what you love to do, the participation and anticipation both give you great satisfaction, getting you more fired up. You're right on target with your life purpose.

Relating to and gradually and appropriately integrating what you love doing most with your life purpose, can give you some tremendous ideas of how to create the life you want. What you most enjoy reflects what you value, and demonstrates how that affects your thinking and resultant behavior.

In the process of working to support your life's purpose, there are certain things you may prefer to avoid or not do, which is true for all of us. At first glance these activities might appear to be in conflict with your life purpose, but they're actually quite necessary for your growth as you forge ahead toward a better life.

53

So why are so many people unhappy with their jobs? It doesn't fully, if at all, support their life purpose and values; therefore, it doesn't fulfill them. If this is true for you, once you realize this, you'll become more hopeful that your life can be improved. You will have discovered a key piece of your life's "puzzle" and, perhaps, the missing piece that, once in place, will enable you to achieve increased happiness and success.

Like millions the world over, you may have chosen to build your own business outside of your job to better your life. Or perhaps you're like those who are already living better lives, but want something more or are looking for a change. You may want the freedom to pursue even bigger goals, perhaps including supporting yourself and your family without having to work a job—*the dream of untold millions more.*

If what you're doing to generate the income you need to pay your bills and live a good life conflicts with your life purpose or values, consider also doing something outside of it that *does* support all of those elements. Perhaps you're already taking advantage of an appropriate additional income vehicle, at least to some extent, if not yet fully.

Whatever the case may be, use an income vehicle that can enable you to create a better life where you *can* transition to living and working more in alignment with your purpose and values. Use doing what you'd rather *not* be doing in your current occupation as a spur to help you stay fired up and take full advantage of that vehicle. Keep your day job until your financial position is such that you absolutely no longer need your job income and benefits and it's wise to consider leaving it. Be sure to consult with your leader, success coach, or mentor and a financial advisor before making such a move.

One Woman's Journey Toward Creating a Better Life

After a few years on the job that she originally thought she'd make a career of, this woman found that it was in conflict with her life purpose. Armed with her new awareness and a heartfelt desire to fulfill her purpose and find more happiness and meaning in life, she started building her own business on the side.

With her new fired-up attitude and the knowledge and skills she's acquired in her business, she longer dreads her job, and has actually become a better employee. She has come to realize that her current occupation is simply a "stepping stone" on her life's journey. Her attitude has shifted dramatically, so much so that her co-workers, and even her boss, have commented on how much more upbeat, happy, and productive she has become.

Knowing her life purpose, values, and preferred activities, she's consistently taking the action necessary to add to her income, with the goal of eventually replacing and exceeding it. This has enabled her to live in integrity with herself and her values, while still working her job and helping to provide for her family.

Getting "The Big Picture"—Increased Awareness Is Powerful

The act of appropriately integrating favorite activities as they relate to life purpose gives greater clarity about the life vision. It starts becoming crystal clear, and engenders enthusiasm and a readiness to move on and make it happen. Perhaps that's where you are right now; if so, congratulations! Fear not. When your vision is clear enough, you'll figure out the "how to do its" along the way.

You now have a vision you can work toward; one that can inspire you to master the principles of success, and a vehicle in which you can apply them in creating a better life. It's likely you're in the best position ever to really make it happen for you and your family.

I'm Fired Up for a Better Life, Principle No. 10—Take Action and Keep Moving

Nothing's ever accomplished without taking action. In order to make things happen, move forward following a proven pattern for success. If you're still unsure about all the details of what a better life means to you, *take action anyway.* Stay in motion and you'll get feedback and clarity as you learn and grow.

You might want to adopt the idea of *ready-fire-aim.* When things go well, you're on track and what you're doing reflects your purpose. If you're not getting the results you may have envisioned, and you're unhappy and out of balance, this is valuable feed back. Learn from it. Then fire again!

Determine what you need to do next, asking for guidance or help when necessary... and go forward. Keep building your business or profession while moving toward a better life—one step at a time, one day at a time.

Those who don't take action stagnate. They sit at home, out of work, on unemployment compensation or welfare, or in an ungratifying dead-end job or career, and they die inside. They complain and refuse to take responsibility for actions that got them where they are, and blame others. They may even throw a "pity party."

But guess what? Nobody shows up! You may know some people like this. Insulate yourself from their negativity. They'll only try to drag you down. By their refusal to move on, they become their own worst enemy.

Doing something worthwhile requires thought and purpose, and often means that person needs to stop feeling sorry for themselves. Until they begin taking positive action, they won't start to truly live or happily fulfill their purpose.

Andrew Shue, the actor, co-founded a nonprofit organization for young people called "Do Something." Young people apply for grants from this organization to do local community projects. Shue's organization has positively influenced many youngsters around the US, and serves as a great role model for others. He believes the bottom line is to take action; to *"Do Something"* so things can get better.

Maybe you've written out your life purpose. You may have developed a short statement describing your dreams, goals, and objectives—explaining exactly how you want to live. If so, that's terrific! You're probably fired up about it. Focus on that statement for a while and see, feel, and hear it happening. After reflection, you may want to change it a bit, and that's fine.

As you're striving for it, your vision of the life you want is always a work in progress. It grows as you grow and become the best you can be. Share it only with your leader or mentor or supportive spouse. This is a deeply personal and private statement and one that may be new and tender to you—like an infant. Protect it and keep it close to your heart, and be sure not to tell negative-thinking people about it. They could be jealous of you and try to douse the flames of your fire.

The immense value of knowing your life purpose is shown in this story. A highly respected, enormously accomplished doctor found that he was getting burned out. He had money and success, but what he really wanted and loved to do was spend time with his family. And since he was working almost all the time to give his wife and children a great lifestyle, he unfortunately was unable to enjoy it with them.

So one day he got fed up, cut back on his medical practice, and started building another business where he could involve his family. In five years, he managed to replace his income, left his medical practice, and now has the time and energy to do what he wants with his family, including periodic medical missions abroad where they all travel and volunteer together. He discovered that life is more rewarding when you live it in line with your purpose.

We all live in accordance with our philosophy of life, which is foundational in determining how we and our lives develop. In sailing, the way the sail is set with respect to the wind determines the direction in which the boat travels. Likewise, the way our mind is set to take advantage of opportunity and cultivate the good that's found in every adversity helps determine our life's direction.

If you don't know exactly what your vision is by now, that's okay. *Keep moving anyway.* Pick a practice objective to use for taking action. It could be something you really want, even though it may not be the ultimate. It might be just one small part of it, or it might be a goal you've had for some time. Choose something that excites you enough to work toward achieving it.

Using this practice objective will give you the chance to learn about taking action with tools that can be applied to anything you may want in life. The important thing is to focus on something positive—*something to aim for.*

If you're not sure what it is, take a moment now to verbalize and write down a practice objective. Start with the two words "I am" and then use "ing" verbs to complete the sentence. (It may help you to review the Life Purpose guidelines in Chapter 7.) Rewrite the sentence until it feels right, keeping it fairly short so you can easily remember it. Once you have it, keep it out in the open where you'll see it often.

Whether you're working with your ultimate or practice objective, you now have a statement which you can focus on and turn into reality. Great! You persisted, created a result, and now have a track to run on. That's what working toward a better life is all about—the process of doggedly persevering, focusing, growing, and taking action on it, as you gradually make it a reality.

Chapter 9

The Dream Fires You Up
to Take Action and Succeed
You Build a Strong Fire with a Solid Plan

"Take action. Do what you can, with what you have,
right where you are. Seize the moment!"
Theodore Roosevelt

The most successful ventures occur with planning and action. Disney World became a reality after Walt flew over the swamps of Florida, envisioning the entire concept. Inspired, Walt went home, developed a plan, assembled a team, and empowered them to take action.

In his imagination, Walt knew what Disney World would look like one, three, five, ten and even twenty years later. He had a magnificent dream for entertaining, uplifting, and educating families in creative fun ways, backed up by a plan for the future. Doing whatever it took in association with others, he and his team made it all a reality.

I'm Fired Up for a Better Life, Principle No. 11—Have a Solid Plan

Now you'll build on your dream for a better life and develop a solid plan for achieving it, as ideas not acted on become unfinished business, causing unnecessary frustration and angst. However, ideas put into practice can result in amazing outcomes, victories, and inventions. The telephone, television, computer, and mobile devices were all the result of ideas put into action, as were the airplane and automobile. And so it is with everything that helps us improve our lives.

None of those inventions would exist if their inventors hadn't had a plan where they continually took action, learned from their mistakes, made adjustments, and kept moving. Now is the time for you to take action toward achieving what you want. As Thomas Edison said... *"The value of an idea lies in the using of it."*

Your Dream for a Better Life Is the Catalyst for Greater Success

While your dream is absolutely essential for you to move ahead and drives you to accomplish more goals, it's *what you become in the process* that's most important. If you were to become wealthy by using people, you'll be disliked, lonely, and unhappy.

However, when you consistently help enough others advance toward achieving *their* dream for a better life, whether their desire is big or small, you can achieve yours; and many will love and respect you along the way.

Here are ten elements showing how pursuing that dream can lead to greater success:

1. The dream for a better life fires us up to take action.

2. In taking action, we overcome fear.

3. In overcoming fear, we develop faith and strength.

4. With faith and strength, we build belief in ourselves.

5. As our belief increases, our confidence grows.

6. With increased confidence, our self-esteem grows.

7. With greater self-esteem we think bigger.

8. Thinking bigger, we realize we can do more by engaging, helping, serving, and empowering others in the quest.

9. As we engage, help, serve, and empower others, we learn and grow through challenges, while taking more action.

10. As we learn and grow through challenges, while taking more action, we accomplish more and achieve greater success.

Consistently apply the above and fine-tune as you go, so you can increasingly get the results which lead to a better life.

Using the *I'm Fired Up for a Better Life*, Action Plan for Dream-Building

This is a valuable tool that you can use over and over again to build a dream and develop a plan for making it a reality. It'll help you get moving in a concrete, practical way. All too often, people have great dreams but never make a plan for achieving them. Cemeteries are full of them, depriving the world of untold great ideas that are never brought to fruition. You don't want that to happen to you. Start *moving* today. A good place to begin is by completing this part of your *action* plan.

Your *I'm Fired Up for a Better Life*, Action Plan for Dream-Building

Name_____

Date_____

"My Dream"—Positively Stated as Choice-Specific, Powerful, and Emotionally Fulfilling

_____

_____

_____

_____

_____

_____

Where I Envision This Dream One, Three, and Five years from Now...

One Year _____

Three Years _____

Five Years _____

Get your notes out from Chapter 7 where you did your life purpose statement. Then fill in the top section above called "My Dream," writing a brief, vivid description of it. State it positively in the present tense, specifically detailing what you're doing and how you're seeing, hearing, and feeling it. Use descriptive words that get you *fired up*. Write it down as clearly as possible, being certain it's something you really want.

Remember, the test for whether you really want something is this: Ask yourself the question: "If I could have it NOW, would I really want it; am I emotionally ready for it?" If the answer is yes, you're ready to put energy into working toward its attainment. If the answer is no or not now, don't put your energy into it. Pursue something that fires you up; a dream that you can embrace right now; something that you really want, that you're emotionally ready for. Otherwise, you'll never do what it takes to achieve it. You've got to feel it in your bones, your heart.

Look over your notes from the process you just did and let your mind go back to what you pictured you were doing and what was happening. Be sure to write it as though it's happening right now. Things you write in future tense almost never happen because they stay mentally in the future. All you have is today; tomorrow is always in the future, promised to no one. Now picture it as if it's happening right *now*—in the present. That makes it come alive for you in your imagination.

Describe the development of your dream one, three, and five years from now as if it's happening now. Pay attention to whatever ideas pop into your head and jot them down in the space provided on the action plan. If you aren't sure how the dream will unfold, just make it up and have fun with it.

What kinds of things would you like to have happening five years from now? Who would you like to be working with? What do you want the quality of your life to be like? Look ahead to three years from now. What do you want to happen by that time? How is your dream developing toward that three-year picture? Then look at one year from now. What actions have you taken? How is that dream growing and taking shape? Remember, at this point you're just playing with ideas; you're not making any commitments. So go ahead and let yourself DREAM BIG, and create a wonderfully fulfilling vision of your better life.

Here's an example of how one person completed the top of the *I'm Fired Up for a Better Life* Action Plan for Dream-Building. In his vision, his new business utilizes his leadership and imagination to work with an excited and cooperative team of associates. As he maps out his one-, three-, and five-year plans, he envisions his business growing steadily from 100 to 1500 to 10,000 people.

He sees himself developing several associates into strong leaders, serving his clients, getting out of debt, gaining financial security and independence, all while helping others do the same. Since he completed the exercise, he has enthusiastically started building his business, following through on his strategic plan.

As you do this, be clear and specific about how you want your dream for a better life to be—feel, look, and sound—one, three, and five years from now. Use your imagination and expand your thinking. Your life could be even better than your current vision allows. It takes enthusiasm...being fired up...as well as planning and consistent diligent action until you make each goal or objective a reality.

Your life may already be exactly how you want it to be in some or maybe many areas, but you might want to make a few adjustments, so you can do more of what you enjoy doing the most. If that's the case, great! Just picture your life exactly as you want it to be, noting where you want to make a change. It may not be a big change; it could be developing enough additional income to reach an educational-fund goal for sending your children to college. Or you may simply want to increase your monthly income to speed up the process of getting out of debt.

If you want to make some significant changes and start living your life with more fulfillment and meaning, while realizing your greatest aspirations, *you can do that too*. The *I'm Fired Up for a Better Life* Action Plan for Dream-Building can help you make your dreams a reality, whatever they may be, as it helps you to focus your mind in the right direction and ramp up your energy to make it happen.

As former US President Andrew Jackson said...

"Take time to deliberate; but when the time for action arrives, stop thinking and GO!"

Chapter 10

Build Your Business or Profession to Live a Better Life
Nurture the Fire So It Never Goes Out

*"Make no little plans; they have no magic to stir
men's blood and probably will not be realized. Make
BIG plans; aim high in hope and work."*
Daniel Hudson Burnham

I deas come to you in a creative way. Have you ever watched a group of small children spontaneously playacting a scene? They gather leaves, for example, transform them into a fort and create fictional characters for each child to act out. Each has input, and they frequently blurt out their ideas as they pop into their heads. What generally results is a highly imaginative, satisfying game that is absorbing and fun. Adults are like that too.

We humans don't create in a linear, organized fashion. While outlining is good for presenting ideas in an orderly, formal manner, it's not all that useful until we've first done the real thinking. Ideas pop in and out of our minds, some of which can take us in entirely new directions. This is where some of your best creative thinking can occur.

As you pursue what you want to accomplish, capturing these creative thoughts is key. Always have a pen and paper or your mobile device handy so you can save your ideas—you never know when they'll show up.

I'm Fired Up for a Better Life, **Principle No. 12—Capture Your Creativity**

A mind map is a great way to organize your thinking and improve productivity by viewing the actions, people, support materials, notes, tools, events, and the like required to build your business or profession. It's a diagram, a "map" that enables you to visualize what you need to do to accomplish something. Mind maps can be done using words, and/or symbols and pictures, to capture many different ideas.

With your main dream, goal, or objective in the center, or hub, several branches radiate out from it in various directions to sub-hubs, with other lines radiating out from them as well, in a tree-branch-like fashion. It can be done the traditional way with a poster board and colored markers, a white board and markers, or digitally with an app for your mobile device or desktop.

Small businesses might use Kraft paper taped over a wall, or a whiteboard, when they're searching for solutions. That way several people can participate and spin off each other's ideas. Corporations use mind maps for planning and flowchart development, as well as project management.

The concept was first popularized by popular psychology author and famous British TV personality Tony Buzan in 1974 who used the term mind map. He had been inspired by Leonardo da Vinci, one of history's greatest thinkers, and his approach to taking notes.

A mind map allows you to capture both your planned and seemingly random "popcorn" ideas quickly and easily. It provides a great springboard to an even more spontaneous imagination. Using it often can help you become a more balanced thinker, utilizing both the emotional and logical sides of your brain as Leonardo did.

Since your mind works in pictures, a mind map will help you visualize the actions or steps you need to take in order to accomplish your aspirations, while you pursue a better life.

Walt Disney used this concept brilliantly with storyboards along with continuous input from his employees. For example, his team used it in creating *The Hunchback of Notre Dame*, one of Disney's top animated films. Various sketches of scenes were laid out on a giant board and the animators would come together to have story meetings, filling in the gaps, rejecting what they could readily see just wouldn't work.

A mind map is a highly effective way of addressing a situation, planning a strategy for new growth, or introducing new products or services. It's also an exceptional tool for helping you create the life you want.

People all over the world, from all walks of life, are building their own businesses to better their lives. The following mind-map creation suggestions, while general in nature, offer some ideas for anyone who has chosen to build their own business.

Map Out the Elements of Building Your Business

Now take out your Action Plan for Dream-Building with the descriptions of what you're doing and how you're seeing, hearing, and feeling it, along with your one-, three-, and five-year statements. Here's what you need to make your mind map using the traditional hand-written paper approach. (Remember, there are apps available for creating a digital mind map.)

- A large piece of paper—either Kraft or construction paper—some people use graph paper. (If you hang your map on a wall as you develop it, put up two layers of paper so the markers don't bleed through to your wall.)

- Colorful felt-tip *non-permanent* markers. Make each major branch a different color and, in some cases, you may want to draw in pictures rather than write words.

- A notebook for recording your ideas and thoughts.

- Artists' white tape or masking tape.

- Your action plan for building your business.

- At least half an hour alone in a quiet place.

Once you have all your tools assembled, look at your action plan, especially the one-, three-, and five-year statements. As you read them you'll get ideas about what actions to take and the results you want, as you work toward improving your life.

First, draw a 2-inch diameter circle in the center of the sheet. Then draw eight main branches radiating out from the circle, evenly spaced around it—north, south, east, west, and half-way between, like on a compass.

Next you're going to label the different branches and sub-branches, letting them come to life on the paper. It's fine if it's busy and crowded—this is strictly for you; you can neaten it up later. Brainstorm as many sub-branches as you can, remembering to group them under main branches as appropriate. Label the main branches in caps; go clockwise starting with the north branch, for example, as follows, with sub-branches connecting to each main branch, also labeled as described below:

1. **North Branch:** PEOPLE I (WE) ALREADY KNOW—**Sub-Branches:** Past Schoolmates, Neighbors (past and present), Co-Workers (past and present), Friends and Relatives, Other Acquaintances.

2. **Northeast Branch:** PRODUCTS AND SERVICES—**Sub-Branches:** Approved Business Apps, Support Materials, Catalogs and Brochures, Web Pages, Samples, Audios and Videos, Demos.

3. **East Branch:** GROWING MY (OUR) ORGANIZATION—**Sub-Branches:** Year One (100 Associates and Clients, 3 Strong Leaders), Year Three (1,500 Associates and Clients, 6 Strong Leaders), Year 5 (10,000 Associates and Clients, 9 Strong Leaders).

4. **Southeast Branch:** MY (OUR) SUCCESS STRATEGY—**Sub-Branches:** Get Fired Up for a Better Life, Define Your Dream, Mission, and Purpose in Life, Set Goals and Commit to Taking Action on Them, Write a List of Prospective Associates, Clients or Customers, Schedule Appointments with the Above People, Give Successful Presentations and Demos, Follow Up with Qualified Prospects, Check Progress and Counsel with Leaders, Share Success Strategy with Others.

5. **South Branch:** POTENTIAL CUSTOMERS OR CLIENTS AND PROSPECTIVE ASSOCIATES—**Sub-Branches:** Family, Friends, Referrals, Neighbors, Parent Groups, Work Contacts, People You Meet Online and Off.

6. **Southwest Branch:** MY (OUR) CONTINUING EDUCATION PROGRAM—**Sub-Branches:** Opportunity Meetings, Corporate Materials, Training Sessions, Corporate and Organizational Online Resources, Conventions, Seminars, Books, Audios, Videos, and Apps.

7. **West Branch:** MY (OUR) LOCATION (House or Apartment)—**Sub-Branches:** Desk/Computer Area, Kitchen or Dining Room Table, Spare Room/Area, Basement/Garage.

8. **Northwest Branch:** MEETING NEW PEOPLE AND STARTING NEW RELATIONSHIPS—**Sub-Branches:** Social Networking, Social Events, Boat Shows, Air Shows, Car Shows, Home Shows, County Fairs, Dream-Building, Trade Shows, Daily Activities.

Ask Questions to Stimulate Your Thinking

Here are some questions to help stimulate you to think of new mind map branches and ideas. (There may be a couple of questions that aren't relevant to your action plan. If so, just ignore them.)

- *What resources or skills* do I need for my action plan?
- *Where* do I want to do my action plan?
- *Who* do I need to contact to make my action plan happen?
- *How* can I reach my one-, three-, and five-year goals?
- *What information* do I need?
- *How much money, if any,* do I need to start my action plan?
- *Who do I know who's successful* at what I'm endeavoring to do that I could ask for business counseling and support?
- *What else* do I need to make my action plan happen?
- What kind of *help* might I need from my family?
- *Who benefits* from my action plan?
- What *needs to change,* that is, be given a different priority, or perhaps be eliminated from my life for me to implement my action plan?

Be Open to the Wealth of Infinite Possibilities

Now that you have a preliminary mind map, you can develop it even more to gain greater insight. Sit down and share it with your mentor or leader. This is the best way to get valuable advice and suggestions, based on your current situation and what's happening in your business or profession. Sharing your mind map is exciting and makes your action plan come alive.

The mind map is to collect ideas and use as a strategic tool. It doesn't represent a commitment, so allow yourself to be as spontaneous as possible when creating it. The time for decisions and commitments is later. This is the time to have fun...*letting your imagination run wild.*

"*Your tongue can light a fire. So share with others and set them on fire with hope and enthusiasm for a better life, stoking your own fire. This will help you stay fired up and keep going where you know you want and need to go.*"

The Publisher

Chapter 11
Make the Most of Your Resources
Start Your Fire with What You Have

*"When every physical and mental resource is focused,
one's power to solve a problem multiplies tremendously."*
Norman Vincent Peale

Webster's Dictionary defines resource as—"a reserve supply of support; something to which one has recourse in difficulty; an ability to meet and handle a situation." Resources can be tangible, like people, books, and audios, or as intangible as peace of mind and happiness. Ranging from legal and financial to educational, spiritual, motivational, and others, resources are essential for helping you achieve what you want.

US Olympic gymnast Kerri Strug made history when she led the women's team to victory. A quiet and barely visible team member until then, she had worked extremely hard to get there. Changing coaches over the years, she finished seventh in the World Championships in Japan.

But she was confused and fearful at that event, and in need of support. So she returned to the rugged training of Bela Karolyi, knowing she'd be second in importance to another gymnast. Kerri's disposition was what concerned her coach the most. Frequently injured and generally high strung, she often had difficulty sleeping.

After rigorous training with Karolyi and an emphasis on *team first*, Kerri led the US team through the first two days of the competition with excellence. Then came the deciding event. Another female gymnast failed at both of her vault attempts. Even though Kerri had injured herself on her first vault, she knew the only way the team could possibly win the gold was for her to do the second vault.

Cheered on by Karolyi, Kerri prayed for help and charged down the runway for an outstanding vault performance. She couldn't even stand up after she was done; her ankle was sprained so badly. But she had done it—she had won the gold medal for her team and her country, and her life would never be the same again.

None of Kerri's success could have occurred without substantial resources. Her coach, team members, and family were her people resources. The funding-for-her-trips resource enabled her to go get the training she needed. And in those last few moments, she turned to God for the inner strength she needed to carry on and triumph. No one, no matter how famous or wealthy, can achieve their aspirations without utilizing resources.

I'm Fired Up for a Better Life, Principle No. 13—Use Your Resources

As you get fired up about your dream for a better life, you may find several resources are required in order to achieve it. So it's best to evaluate exactly what resources you currently have and those you may need to develop.

Later in this chapter is an example of a resource list for starting your own business. Divided into 11 categories, there are specific resources suggested, and there could be some other resources under each one of those. This list is just an example and isn't meant to be official or comprehensive.

Consider a married couple who owned a farm. Tired of getting up so early and working so hard, they wanted to change their way of life. In order to make the transition, they started another business. Having done well in farming, they really didn't need any financial resources. However, they did have need of the following:

1. Start-up kit and optional tools.

2. Continuing Education—to get training in personal, professional, and leadership development, as well as people skills.

3. Prospecting—to help them bring people into their organization to be associated business owners, as well as to find others to be members, and customers or clients.

They didn't need any employees, buildings, or manufacturing equipment. Instead, they found and chose to build a business that was fairly simple and economical. It also provided them with the venues to associate with and learn from other nice people, which was really important to them.

I'm Fired Up for a Better Life, Principle No. 14—Connect with the Right People

When you begin the quest for improving your life, start meeting and associating with like-minded people. You don't have to figure out and do everything alone. There are people who can guide and even help you do what you want to do.

Rather than reinventing the wheel, learn from those who are where you want to be. Duplicating their pattern or method of success can save you from making a lot of unnecessary mistakes, helping you succeed. Asking about and taking advantage of the information and tools already available from others is a smart thing to do. You may not know where the answer to one of your challenges will come from.

You may not know who has the contact who will lead you to the next leader in your business or profession. On average, we're all only about seven people away from anyone in the world. It would take a chain of only seven contacts to reach the president of a country or well-known CEO, or anyone else who now seems unreachable.

The key is to make a list of people you can contact, then start taking action. You may be better connected than you think. Statistics show that, on average, most people know about 250 other people. People are our greatest resource. People are first; products and services follow. Go through the noes to connect with the right people who agree with you, are interested in learning more about your product, service, or your opportunity if they have a desire to better their lives.

As you meet people and make new friends, remember what Dale Carnegie said... *"You can make more friends in two months by becoming more interested in others than you can in two years by trying to get them interested in you."*

Sometimes the best way others can help you is to believe in you and your ability to achieve what you want. As in any quest, your success coach, leader, or mentor shows they believe in you by encouraging and being supportive of you and your efforts in building your business or profession. You can then pass this belief on to others and help them achieve what they want. From a tiny spark, the flames of enthusiasm can spread very quickly.

Contrary to popular belief, no one is self-made. It takes the cooperation of other people to accomplish anything of significance. No one can become successful alone, no matter what field of endeavor they may be in. The most effective and efficient way anyone can succeed is to help others succeed. Be committed to empowering and helping others, and good things will happen in your life.

Use the *I'm Fired Up for a Better Life* Action Plan with Resources

Focus on your Action Plan, investing about ten minutes reviewing the resources you already have (like motivation and contacts), and those you need to develop (like a relationship with your leader, success coach, or mentor, or time/activity management).

What specific results would you like to see from pursuing your aspirations for a better life? You may simply want to get out of debt while working your job. Or perhaps you want to transition to retiring from your full- or part-time job or current profession so you can eventually devote full-time to your new venture.

What strengths do you need to build on in order to be more successful? Maybe it's learning to ignore negative-thinking people who are putting you or what you're doing down, or trying to dissuade you from wanting to improve your life. Carefully consider each of your answers. They'll be useful in helping you decide which action steps to take next... so you can make progress.

You may still need several more resources. Do whatever it takes to get what you need to build your business or profession so you can make your desired new life situation a reality. Take advantage of the system of success available to you and encourage your associates to do the same. Remember, you're investing in yourself.

When you're passionate, committed, and fired up, and sharing your enthusiasm with others, people will come into your life who believe in you and what you're doing. And by helping them achieve what they want you can achieve what you want. It's a well- known fact of success that the more people you help achieve what they want, the more you'll achieve what you want. It's simply impossible to be successful alone.

When you have a big enough desire and vision for your future, you can overcome whatever obstacles you encounter.

Sample Resource List for Starting and Building Your Own Business

Business Ownership Plan

-Relationships
-Presentation Supplies
-Prospecting Tools

-Sample Products
-Catalogs, Brochures, Apps
-Web Site(s), Audios, Videos

Legal

-Business Agreement
-Code of Ethics

-Supplier Corp. By-Laws
 and Rules of Conduct

Financial

-Start-up Kit Cost

-Checkbook, Credit/Debit Card

Location and Supplies

-Home Office/Kitchen Table
-Office Equipment and Supplies

-Computer/Mobile Device
-Books, Audios, Videos

Education and Training

-One-on-One Counseling
-Books, Audios, and Videos
-Seminars and Conventions

-Training Sessions
-Other Leadership Events
-Publications and Apps

Personal Support Structure

-Mentor, Leader, Success Coach
-Business Associates
-Social Media Friends

-Positive-Thinking Family,
 Friends, and Acquaintances

Motivation and Inspiration

-Books, Audios, Videos
-Seminars and Conventions
-Dream-Building Sessions

-Training Sessions and
 other Leadership Events

Time/Activity Management

-Planner or Mobile Device/App
-Balancing Home, Work,
 and Business

-Goal Setting, Planning
-Scheduling and Organizing

Health—Physical and Mental

-Diet and Nutrition
-Vitamins and Supplements

-Exercise and Rest
-Positive Attitude

Spiritual

-Inspirational Reading

-Prayer, Meditation, Faith

Strengths to Be Developed for Accomplishing My Objective

1._____

2._____

3._____

Resources I Have

1._____

2._____

3._____

Resources I Need

1._____

2._____

3_____

Chapter 12
What About Money?
Maintain a Constant Supply of Fuel

*"Improve your financial situation so you can live a better
life. Live below your means, build a secondary income, get
out of debt, and share what you're doing with others."*
The Publisher

Persist so you can reap the rewards, and use your creativity to develop financial resources when working toward bettering your life. For example, some people who are serious about improving their lives will even sell one of their distracting, time-wasting household items, for example, a TV, to get some money to move on.

On the other hand, those not committed to creating a better life will hold on to and continue using such time-wasters, blaming their lack of financial resources as an excuse not to do something. They're, perhaps inadvertently, choosing to stay stuck. How about you? Do you have the attitude that nothing is going to get in the way of your quest? That's what champions believe; doing whatever it takes.

Even though the US is the wealthiest country in the world, there are still homeless, starving people. And most who are gainfully employed still operate from a philosophy of not being able to improve their situation. This is poverty thinking, and it's fueled by debt, the obsession with credit card spending, and living beyond their means.

This level of thinking has a built-in negative belief system that says, "There's not enough for everyone, therefore there's not enough for me to have a better life. So why bother trying to get ahead?" This is a limiting belief and it's false. It's very different from prosperity thinking which says there's more than enough for everyone, and that we're all capable of honorably improving our lives and enjoying the additional fruits of our labor... and then sharing that liberating belief with others.

Be sure you're thinking prosperity rather than poverty. It makes a huge difference in how convinced you are of your possibilities for a brighter future. It also affects how much you believe you can do it which is essential before you can go on to achieve your desired new level of living.

As former US President Harry S. Truman said...

"There's enough in the world for everyone to have plenty to live on happily and to be at peace with his neighbors."

Fortunately, there are excellent books and techniques to help change a broke focus to one of wealth and freedom. There are books available that have effective suggestions and tools for overcoming debt and cultivating wealth.

It's absolutely essential for you to get out of debt and live within your means so you can build your wealth. Check with your success coach, leader, or mentor and ask what books they might recommend for you to read.

When you realize that wealth is so much more than money, you'll get fired up about how truly wealthy you already are. When you're grateful for all the blessings you already have in your life, it increases your possibilities of receiving more.

Always maintain an attitude of gratitude.

I'm Fired Up for a Better Life, Principle No. 15—Manage Your Money and Get Out of Debt

Another reason why people sometimes struggle financially is because they feel *unworthy* of success or wealth. Again, myths from earlier in life can hold you back today—*but only if you let them*. If you haven't yet done so, it's time to expose and let go of these myths, as covered in Chapter 6. Such myths are often deeply ingrained in the subconscious and have a powerful hold on people—*until they let them go*.

You can tell if you need to uncover more myths by noticing where you may be stuck. Ask yourself, "What have I been striving to do financially where I've been unsuccessful? What do I believe that may be false and holding me back from achieving my goals?"

For example, back when I was single, I used to think that if I owned a beautiful home, I'd never get married. But since I really wanted to be happily married, I recognized this myth for what it was, let it go and, as mentioned, built a beautiful house by the river. Starting out as just a slab of concrete, week after week I watched it grow into the lovely home which became my tranquil refuge. A year and a half after I moved in, I met my then-future husband, who fell in love with the house soon after he fell in love with me!

To uncover any money myths that may be holding you back from improving your financial situation and the life you long for, invest a few minutes in the following activity.

Eliminating Money Myths Activity

Get a recorder or your mobile device and give yourself 15 minutes alone in a quiet place. Start freely talking or writing how you feel about money. Start with statements like "Money is...," or "I think money is...," or "From the viewpoint of my father, money is...," "From the viewpoint of my mother, money is...," "In the eyes of my faith, money is...," "From the perspective of my business or profession, money is...," and let yourself ramble on. Pour out any thoughts which come to mind about money. After you're through, take a break.

Come back in a half-hour and listen to or read what you said or wrote. Notice any limiting beliefs that you may have about money.

For instance, many people mistakenly believe that the Bible says that "money is the root of all evil." But what it really says is that "the *love* of money is *a* root of evil." Money *is just a tool*—a medium of exchange, a way of keeping score—and it's neutral. It's neither good nor bad, it's compensation for services rendered, and it's used to do good things when in the hands of good people.

Money is the only thing that can do what it does. It builds homes, churches, schools, hospitals, colleges, universities, and other buildings. It puts a roof over your head, clothes on your back, and food on your table. More good people like you need to be earning more income so more good can be done in the world.

List all your myths and study them. You may discover something that has prevented you from enjoying greater financial security up until now. Then, draw an "X" through the page and tear up the paper, delete the words, or eliminate the recording, as a symbol of your letting go of those myths. With your new awareness, they won't hold you back anymore. Congratulations! You've just created an open space, a vacuum, in your mind to receive wealth-inducing ideas. Since nature abhors a vacuum, fill your mind with ideas that will support you in your quest of achieving your financial goals.

Here are a few key ideas to help you improve your financial situation relative to your monthly spending and credit card usage. Let these get you fired up about getting rid of debt and building your wealth.

Money Tip No. 1—*Credit Cards.* Credit cards are often recommended as a convenience, with many people carrying them instead of cash. Just be sure to pay off the balance every month to avoid paying the outrageous interest. A helpful technique is to *record every credit card purchase in your checkbook or digital ledger and subtract it from the balance.* Put a little box or star around it so you know it's a credit card expense and not a check. Then when the bill comes in, you already have the money set aside to pay for those purchases. You won't be increasing your debt or incurring any finance charges, and you'll start each month with a zero credit card balance.

Money Tip No. 2—*Debit Cards.* You may want to use a debit card, which automatically withdraws cash directly from your checking account as you spend it. This is a safer method than a credit card because you can spend only what you have in that account. It helps to record the amount you spend, along with any fee, with your debit card in your mobile device on the date you spend it if you don't have your checkbook with you. But remember to record your usage in your checkbook, so you always know how much money is in your account.

Money Tip No. 3—*Lower Interest Rates and No Annual Fees.* There are many ways to *cut down* on credit card interest and *eliminate* annual fees as you *pay off* any credit card debt you may have accumulated. Interest rates and annual fee practices vary a great deal from bank to bank. Most people don't question these costs, not realizing that this mistake could cost them hundreds, and possibly even thousands, of dollars a year.

Many years ago I had an experience with a credit card company that may benefit you. I received a notice in the mail that they had increased my line of credit by $4000 at a low interest rate. I called to verify that this was not a short-term "trick" offer and then I asked, "If I use the increased credit line to pay off other credit cards, what would my rate be?" They reviewed my credit history and permanently lowered the interest rate on the entire balance on the card, including for the new $4000 line. Delighted, I decided to pursue getting my other card rates lowered too. As it turned out, half of them lowered my rate, which ended up saving me hundreds of dollars in interest that year.

You can do it too. Ask to speak to someone in customer service for each of the companies and banks you deal with, and tell them you're looking for the best deal among all your credit card providers. Ask each one if you can get a better interest rate along with no annual fee, if you would shift all of your credit card debt and other banking business to them. You'll be happy to discover that you can often get a better deal just by asking! Keep asking for what you want. Once you get that deal, be sure to pay off the debt as quickly as possible.

Money Tip No. 4—*The Freezer Fix Approach.* Whenever you go shopping, leave all your credit cards at home, so you can't possibly be tempted to spend money you don't have. Also, avoid TV or Internet shopping. You can impulsively spend lots of money on things you really don't need by getting caught up in an infomercial, home shopping show, or enticing on-line offers. Another idea is to take all your credit cards and freeze them in a block of ice, so it's difficult to use them. Or you could even keep the credit card with the best interest rate, and cut up the rest and throw them away. Either way, buy only what you absolutely need.

Money Tip No. 5—*Consolidation Loans? Buyer Beware.* It's likely you've seen finance companies' advertisements that promise to consolidate your debt into one loan, at less interest and smaller monthly payments. They often try to make their offer seem even more attractive by lending you *more* money than you need.

Two things generally result when people borrow from such companies:

1. They borrow more money and get even deeper in debt for a longer period of time.

2. With their new paid-off credit cards, instead of closing the accounts, they continue their charging habit. They often charge until they load up again to their credit limit.

So not only are these people no better for their consolidation loan, they're usually worse off! They could jeopardize their family's finances to where they may lose everything and even go bankrupt.

Be very suspect of those too-good-to-be-true sounding ads. They usually are. A well-thought-out plan to pay off those credit card accounts and your other loans, too, is a better bet. For example, get all your credit card debt onto one or two cards with the lowest interest rates. Also, look for cards with the lowest or no annual fees, and pay off as much as you possibly can that's over the minimum each month.

Being debt-free is one of the best goals you can have. Debt drains your energy and drags you down. Having no debt frees you up and gets you fired up. Persist until you pay off your credit cards and eliminate credit card interest altogether. It's worth it.

"Make it a point to do something every day that you don't want to do. This is the golden rule for acquiring the habit of doing what we need to do without pain."

Mark Twain

Chapter 13
Make Each Day Count
Consistently Fan the Flames for More Heat

"Make every day of your life count... live peacefully, happily, and successfully by reading the right materials, meeting the right people, and doing utmost good for yourself and mankind."
Isaac Idakwo

As you stay fired up in pursuing a better life, you'll soon discover that one of the best ways to support yourself in making progress toward it is by making each day count through effective use of your time.

I'm Fired Up for a Better Life, Principle No. 16—Use Your Time Wisely

You may already be using a paper system or an app for time/activity management. Perhaps you've even taken a course or attended a seminar for helping you get organized and accomplish more. That's great! But regardless, here's an interesting perspective for you to consider as you build your business or profession and balance your other priorities too.

Bestselling author and speaker, the late Dr. Stephen R. Covey shared an attention-grabbing story which went something like this: In a lecture one time, the instructor said...

"We're now going to have a quiz." He pulled out a wide-mouth gallon jar and several fist-size rocks, asking the class, "How many of these rocks do you think we can get into the jar?"

After many guesses from his students, he began to put the rocks into the jar until no more would fit in. He then asked, "Is the jar full?" The class responded, "Yes."

The instructor then said, "Aah—wait," and took a bucket of gravel and dumped as much as he could into the jar. The gravel, of course, filled some of the spaces left by the big rocks.

He then asked again, "Is the jar full?" By this time the class was beginning to understand the lesson he was teaching. "Probably not," they replied. "Good," the instructor said, as he brought out a bucket of sand. He dumped as much as he could into the jar, and it began filling all the crevices left by the rocks and the gravel.

He asked once more, "Is the jar full?" "No!" said the class enthusiastically. He then took a quart of water and poured as much of it as he could into the jar, completely saturating all the little crevices between the grains of sand, gravel, and rocks.

"The point is," he said, "if you hadn't put the big rocks in first, you would never have gotten any of them into the jar."

Many people try to cram way too much sand, gravel, and water into their lives without investing time to schedule-in the "big rocks." The big rocks represent what's most important in your life.

In Chapter 7 you examined what your values are and what's truly most meaningful to you. In the next activity, you'll have the opportunity to refine your list even more by identifying and focusing on your top priorities.

This activity is quite worthwhile, because once you know what your big rocks are you can set up your entire time/activity management program around what's really most important to you. It means *you* are in control of your life—*not* the outside world. Consciously making your own choices helps you to stay fired up about your life. This is key. You won't allow any distractions to interfere or throw you off track. You always stay on task, on purpose.

The Big Rocks Activity

Take a few minutes now to make a list of those things in your life that are most important to you. Don't be concerned about the order you put them in; just quickly write them out as they come to mind. Here are some examples—*spiritual, spouse, children, health, having a better life, job, business.*

Once you've made the list, rank the items in their order of priority. Now you know which ones to put first on your calendar or planner, or in your to-do, getting-things-done, or appointment app.

Look over what you've got going next week and schedule in time for each big rock listed, giving special priority to rocks 1-5. When you schedule your big rocks first, you'll attend to the most important things in your life... and feel happier, more fulfilled, and fired up. This is a significantly different approach than most traditional time/activity management/planning systems, which have you scheduling according to critical deadlines and other's agendas.

Compromises may be necessary, especially if you work for someone else. But it's much easier to talk to your boss about other options, rather than working late on a particular night, if you've already logged a commitment in your schedule. You could say something like this to your boss...

"I'm busy tonight after work. If I had known about this sooner, I would have rearranged my schedule. However, I'll be happy to come in early or stay late tomorrow. Would that be okay with you?"

Most of the time an understanding boss would probably accept that approach... as long as your request is clear and reasonable and gives them some other options. They're also likely to respect you more because you're showing respect for yourself and your family. Yet you're doing it in an inoffensive way, intent on making it a win-win situation.

So, in addition to using the big-rocks approach, *how else can you better use your time?* Here are some time tips to help you stay fired up and on-target as you strive for a better life.

Time Tip No. 1—*Get an Excellent Time/Activity Management System or App.* While some people use a paper-based system, most use an electronic one or perhaps a combination of both. But no matter what kind of system you use, take it everywhere you go. Whenever you have a thought about something which needs to be done, you can capture and/or schedule it. Otherwise, you're likely to forget something important. Busy people need to be organized.

Many years ago, I took a sales course in which we were given a test to measure our sales abilities. I did well on the test, except for one area—time/activity management. The instructor emphasized how important it is to get a good time/activity management system to track everything you're doing and enter all your creative ideas. That convinced me to get a system right there and then.

Choose a system or app that really appeals to you, and make sure you use it every day. The simple act of doing so makes many people feel more successful. That, alone, is a great benefit.

Time Tip No. 2—*Using Your Time/Activity Management System or App.* Be sure to enter all commitments and agreements into it, labeling or highlighting each big-rock activity accordingly. In the process, remember that broken agreements destroy relationships and damage your self-esteem. *Keep your promises with yourself, as well as those made to others,* by entering and prioritizing them and then taking appropriate action.

Also be sure to include a file for your better life dream, and enter any relevant items like your mind map, goals, objectives, and action plan. Also set up all your addresses, phone numbers, emails, social media contact information, for work, business, and personal, so you can easily get to them at all times. Include any pertinent details like co-worker, associate, prospect, client, and customer lists; birthdates, anniversaries, and other key information you may want to remember.

One thing that might be going through your mind is, "What happens if I lose my system or mobile device?" The answer is, don't! Make it a top priority to hang on to it.

Many years ago, my husband lost his paper-based system on Christmas Eve. He left it in a shopping cart at a grocery store parking lot, not realizing it was missing until he got home. He went back to the store, but it was gone. Being such a goal-oriented person, he wanted to order another one that night to replace it, but I suggested he wait. After all, it was Christmas Eve and I was certain someone would return it to him. Sure enough, later that night, the local post office called and said someone had turned it in. A postman delivered it to us on Christmas morning! Talk about caring service.

Time Tip No. 3—*Minimize and Fine-Tune Your "To Do" Lists.* Here's a question for you. How often do you get to the end of the day and discover there are still things to be done that are on your to do list? When I ask seminar groups this question, most people raise their hand. How does that feel? Not very good.

It's best to write down and prioritize only what you can reasonably expect to do in a day, allowing time for the unexpected challenges that often seem to occur. Then, as you check off what you've done that day, you can feel good about it. You can choose to move anything undone to another day, decide it's no longer a priority, or perhaps it doesn't need to be done at all, for whatever reason.

To keep yourself on track with your business or profession, enter the dates and times into your time/activity management system or app of meetings, seminars, conventions, training sessions, webinars, telecons, tele-seminars, and any other special events that are in your best interest to participate in or attend. The easiest thing to do is put these in your calendar as soon as your learn about them, at the start of every month, and later as needed. Do this as soon as you become aware of places you need to go, people you need to see or communicate with, and things you need to do.

Reschedule anything you must in order to take full advantage of whatever activities will help you move ahead. This is one of the most important ways you can stay focused and fired up to make your dream a reality. You'll also be a good empowering example to others as you grow in your leadership ability and take on more responsibilities.

Time Tip No. 4—*Create Daily Success Lists.* If you don't have a time/activity management system or app yet, use a notebook or your computer or mobile device. At the end of every day, write out at least ten successes, big or small, you had that day.

Some people may judge themselves negatively and say they had no success. But every positive action you take, no matter how small, is a success—you did *something* toward achieving your goal. Movement is the key. Every communication you made to an associate, prospect, customer, or client is a success, regardless of how they responded. Every time you make a presentation it's a success, whether the prospect(s) is interested or not.

Whether you got the outcome you wanted or not, you took positive action and such action is always somehow rewarded. In some cases, the reward is that you learned something valuable you can use later—like what *not* to do! Or perhaps you did something you were afraid to do and you've increased your confidence as a result.

Regardless of what happens, keep going because it will help you stay fired up. If you don't take action, you'll frustrate yourself because you don't even give yourself the chance that you'll get the results you say you want. Successful people persist until they reach their goal, and then keep persisting—they don't give up. They build momentum toward achieving their objective. Stopping, only having to start again, kills any momentum that could have been created and sustained.

For instance, many successful businesspeople believe that for every ten noes they receive, they get one yes. In fact, they actually thank the noes enthusiastically, at least in their minds, because that puts them one step closer to a yes. They understand that following their business's or industry's success system, while continually taking action doing whatever it takes, is key to growing their business or profession.

You may not be able to complete on some of the things you're working on in any given day, but you took action and that's a win. For example, you've scheduled some presentations but have yet to confirm them. Let's face it, some days just getting out of bed and going to work is a success, particularly if you don't feel like it!

Consistently tracking your successes gives you an amazing boost to your self-esteem. You'll know you're making progress.

I had a wonderful experience with this in a course I took. Part of our weekly assignment was to record our successes which made a surprising difference to me. I did it for about 300 days that year, and when I looked back at the record at the end of the year, I saw how much I had accomplished. It said to me, "You're a person who gets things done; and you're successful and effective." I was fired up about my ability to achieve. I know it may seem silly, but it works. Do it for at least two months and see for yourself. When you look back over all that you've done, you'll probably find that you do a great deal and you're a winner.

Time Tip No. 5—*Live in the Present.* Far too many people make the mistake of wasting time thinking about things that have happened or worrying about things that could happen. They're often mentally reliving the good old days or projecting their lives too far in the future, missing the present. The truly successful know that the only time we have is now, so they make the most of each moment. When you're living in the present, you're in your most resourceful and productive state. It's the only time you can take action.

While you keep your vision of a better life in front of you, do what you can today (and every day) toward achieving it, enjoying the experience of appreciating and living in the present. Forget yesterday; it's over and done with. Focus on what you can do right now, in this very moment. Make each day count, giving priority daily to wisely investing your time in incrementally working toward reaching your objectives. You'll be glad you did!

By living every moment fully in the present, you can take action, get results, and triumph. Be fired up and your better life vision will become more alive in your mind and heart, more believable, and therefore more achievable.

Chapter 14
Upgrade Your Vitality
Continuously Breathe New Life into Your Fire

"Developing and maintaining healthy habits is essential.
They'll give you the stamina to work toward living a better
life, and the energy to enjoy what you've earned."
The Publisher

Living life is much more difficult without good health. Your physical and mental health are important resources for achieving a better life. Feeling good physically and mentally helps keep you fired up.

I'm Fired Up for a Better Life, **Principle No. 17—Take Care of Your Health**

Unfortunately, good health is a resource many people tend to overlook and take for granted. Are you health habits supporting you in living a better life or detracting from it?

I witnessed how poor health can destroy a person's life through my mother's long-term illness and subsequent death. I saw a brilliant, artistic, beautiful woman disintegrate into a jaundiced, frail shell of a human being in constant pain.

After 15 years of being in and out hospitals, at 45 my mother sadly passed away... much too soon. Her illness and death significantly colored my life and health choices. As I have grown older, I've learned to take good care of myself. That starts first with a healthy, balanced diet, followed by regular, fun exercise and relaxation. I prefer to be as natural in my approach to health as possible. Here are five tips for healthy living.

Health Tip No. 1—*Take Vitamins, Minerals, and Antioxidants.* Certainly, a well-balanced diet is the best source of excellent nutrition, but because of extensive food processing, the next best sources are vitamins, minerals, antioxidants, and other supplements. Read about them and do what is best for you. Invest in your health, and improve the quality of your life.

Health Tip No. 2—*Exercise Four-to-Five Times a Week.* The latest research shows that 30 minutes of exercise that gets your heart rate up at least four times a week, can add years to your life. Find an activity, like brisk walking, that you can do wherever you are. All you need is comfortable sneakers or walking shoes.

You could even listen to audios as you walk and get both physically and mentally fired up at the same time. You could also do some stretching and toning exercises with light weights, such as sit-ups and leg lifts. Just be sure to consult with your physician before you embark on any exercise program.

Health Tip No. 3—*Eat Four to Five Fruit and Vegetable Servings a Day.* The various diet and nutrition books on the market all suggest eating lots of fruits and vegetables, while cutting down on sugar, fats, and salt. It's easy to work four or five servings of fruits and vegetables into your day when you plan it by including juice, fruits, and raw vegetables, like carrots, as snacks.

Health Tip No. 4—*Drink Lots of Water.* This is another tip most of us have heard for a long time. But now, more than ever, as you're in pursuit of a better life, it's important to drink plenty of water to help keep you hydrated, fit, and fired up.

We've all heard the advice to drink at least eight 8-ounce glasses of water a day. According to the Mayo Clinic, "That's about 1.9 liters, which isn't that different from the Institute of Medicine recommendations. Although the '8 by 8' rule isn't supported by hard evidence, it remains popular because it's easy to remember. Just keep in mind that it could be reframed as: 'Drink at least eight 8-ounce glasses of fluid a day,' as all fluids count toward the daily total.

The great thing about water is that it not only fills you up without calories, but also flushes out toxins and can help your skin be more elastic and younger looking. To assure the purity of your water, you could install a simple under-the-sink water treatment system for your drinking and cooking needs. In addition to providing you with healthier water, it'll save you money over buying bottled water.

Health Tip No. 5—*Get Enough Rest.* Daily sleep requirements vary. You need less when you're fired up, eat properly, exercise, and take food supplements. When you're running hard for a goal and sleep less than you normally would, a 20-30 minute nap in the late afternoon or early evening can help.

Before you fall asleep and when you wake up, focus on your vision for a better life. Your mind is more relaxed and receptive right before you go to sleep and when you first awake, making it easier for your subconscious to work on it. It's like planting a seed in fertile soil, helping you stay fired up, focused, and on track. Putting pictures of your envisioned life on the wall by your bed helps with this process.

I'm Fired Up for a Better Life, **Principle No. 18—*Laugh About It***
Laughter is one of the most powerful ingredients for good health. Take yourself lightly and your aspirations seriously... and laugh at your own mistakes. This helps you take challenges in stride, while maintaining a positive attitude. Buy a clean joke or riddle book. Carry it with you, either in paper form or electronically in your mobile device, or you could write down some of the jokes and riddles. Be sure to share them with others to help lighten their loads as well as your own.

Also, look for the humor in everyday events. Have you ever had the experience of pure fun and laughter when you're with family, friends, and associates? Have you ever felt the freeing feeling of a very deep belly laugh? That laughter releases endorphins and makes you feel good. Laughter helps you to relax your system and gets the energy flowing inside you. It gets you fired up.

I'm Fired Up for a Better Life, **Principle No. 19—*Your Dream for a Better Life Can Help You Recover from Illness or Injury***
Another aid in recovering from illness or injury is the power of the dream. The hope engendered by the dream for a better life can

help you deal with health challenges. This has been true for countless athletes who've triumphed over serious injuries.

Joan Benoit, renowned Olympic marathon runner, had surgery done on both Achilles tendons. Seemingly recovered, she began preparing for the Olympics. Only two months before the trials, she had severe pain in her right knee, which slowed down her running. For a while, her doctor injected cortisone into her knees. But the pain returned to such an extent that she could barely walk.

Courageously, Benoit took a major risk. With only 17 days to go before the Olympic trials, she underwent arthroscopic surgery. Afterward, she felt no pain. But later on, she overcompensated with her left leg, hurting her hamstring. After her initial uncertainty, she decided to start the trials and see how far she could go. Not only did she make the trials, she excelled, leading the pack of runners on a 26-mile Olympic marathon. She made medical and sports history and took the gold medal. Her dream got her fired up and led her to victory.

Take care of your health. Get and keep your body as sound as possible and maintain a positive attitude. This will support you as you create your better life. Having vitality and optimism makes it easier to stay fired up and do what's required to reach your objectives. Focusing on good health is a great way to do that. Do the best you can with what you have in this area.

If you have a major physical or mental challenge, you can still take good care of yourself, rouse your enthusiasm, and move on to a better life. As bestselling author Napoleon Hill said...

"Every adversity, every failure, every heartache carries with it the seed of an equal or greater benefit."

Chapter 15

Maintaining a Positive Attitude Is Essential for a Better Life

Feeding the Fire Inside of You

*"Every great and commanding movement in
the annals of the world is the triumph of enthusiasm.
Nothing great was ever achieved without it."*
Ralph Waldo Emerson

How's your attitude? In 1914 Thomas Edison, one of the world's great thinkers, faced a very difficult challenge. His laboratory and all the work inside it caught fire and burned to the ground. Instead of being dismayed and quitting, like so many people would have done when faced with such a great adversity, he said...

"All the mistakes are burned up. Thank God we can start anew!"

That's the mark of a true optimist—one who faces the world with a positive perspective, no matter what the circumstance or challenge may be. Having a positive attitude is essential in maintaining enthusiasm for a better life, and staying fired up enough to achieve it.

What Happens *to* You Happens *for* You

Your attitude is completely within your control; it's one of the few things in life that is. It's simply a choice, and you can change it at any time. Bestselling author and speaker, the late Alan Loy

McGinnis concluded that, after studying the lives of thousands of successful people: "The road to a happy and successful life is paved with optimism." That's not to say life won't provide you with challenges nor that you should ignore the difficulties that present themselves along the way. Inside every one is a solution and a lesson. Understand that *what happens to you happens for you.* Always look for the good in everything and *grow through* the experience instead of just *going through* it like most.

It's easy to be positive when things are going well. But when you encounter an obstacle—now *that's* where the true test of your attitude comes in. How you view and handle a particular situation is your choice; you can become negative and pessimistic and just complain, or you can look for the solutions and draw on your available resources. Each situation is an opportunity in disguise—to learn and grow—a chance to become the best you can be. In overcoming and rising above the obstacle you gain wisdom, along with the increased strength and confidence you need to continue.

Growing in a Foreign Country

I know, first-hand, how important attitude is. When I was 16, I went to live in Kingston, Jamaica with a Jamaican family I had met a few years earlier. As part of my senior project in school, I volunteered to teach English there for a month. Even though I had tutored throughout high school, I wasn't expecting these junior high school classes in Kingston to be so large. There were 45 students in one class, 65 in another. Classes were conducted in concrete rooms with one wall open to let the air in.

Their rigorous school discipline also surprised me. Hearing a loud noise one day, I rushed outside to see what was happening. I ran to break up what I thought was a fight between two students, only to find the children cheering as a teacher was beating a boy who had been unruly. I was shocked. In the early 1970s Jamaican schools still maintained the British tradition of corporal punishment. That day lead to a turning point in my attitude. In spite of my fear, I decided to make a bigger difference in the lives of my students by teaching them self-discipline.

Fired up about my chance to make a contribution, I spent time with my students on a personal level. I took them on a field trip to the zoo *right next door;* something that had never been done! I got to know my students as people and learned that a lot of them never had money for lunch or even milk. The children were bright and hungry to learn about the world, but many would never get beyond ninth grade. They would then go to work to support their families or become farmers. But they still wanted to reach out, so they became pen pals to my students in the US.

My experience at this Jamaican school made quite an impression on me. Many of the teachers there were optimistic and hopeful; they welcomed me and shared their stories with me. I learned that no matter what the system is or the rules are—*one person with a positive attitude can make a difference.*

I was so excited that I did my thesis on Jamaican education. I returned there several times while in college, and later, to do more research. I learned a great deal about myself and others, and grew wiser from my time there. I'm pleased to report Jamaican education has improved significantly since that time, and there's more hope for the children there today.

As you're bettering your life, you may find delays in the process, times when things don't go smoothly and doors get slammed in your face. That's the point at which to draw on your inner resources, keep the faith, and rekindle your sparks inside. It's always an internal choice.

You never know what good fortune will come out of adversity. At a minimum, you can learn and grow from it, making you stronger and more capable of handling future challenges. As you go, your understanding and compassion for others will deepen, enabling you to be an optimistic servant-leader of the finest caliber.

Julio Iglesias was a professional soccer player in Madrid, living his dream life as he knew it at the time. But one fateful day he was severely injured, paralyzed from an automobile accident. He spent a long time in the hospital, and while there, a nurse gave him a guitar. Little did she know she was launching the career of one of the world's most successful popular singers. What if Julio hadn't had the adversity of that "accident"? Everything happens for a reason.

I'm Fired Up for a Better Life, Principle No. 20—Go from "It Could Happen" to "It Will Happen!"

In the popular Disney film *Angels in the Outfield*, there's a cute, friendly little boy, JP, who lives in a foster home. His mother was homeless and had been raising him in the front seat of their car. But in spite of his experience, JP never gave up hope that his mother would come back and get him, or that some loving person would adopt him. The philosophy of his young life was summed up in a wistful phrase, which he repeats over and over to himself and others throughout the movie... *"It could happen."*

That line is key to the theme of the movie and what happens to JP and Roger, the movie's main character, who also lives in the foster home. In the end, JP gets his wish—his dream for a better life comes true. A caring man, the coach of the Angels baseball team, happily adopts both of the boys. JP's philosophy of *"It could happen"* paid off.

Be open-minded and anticipate that, as long as you persist, good things can happen to you that can also lead you to improving your life. As you follow in the footsteps of your success coach, leader, or mentor, doors once closed will open, and all sorts of miracles can take place. A good way to start is by adopting little JP's it-could-happen philosophy, and then changing it to "It will happen!" in order to maximize your potential to better your life. Then put your heart and soul into it.

I'm Fired Up for a Better Life, Principle No. 21—Don't Be Attached to Any Particular Person or Outcome

One of the ways that can help your life improve—right now—is not to be attached to any particular person or outcome, while maintaining a positive focus on your objective and continuing to do whatever it takes to achieve it.

Some people may want to improve their lives so desperately that they push too hard and alienate others. They're so mentally attached to it that they aggressively try to force it to happen, which actually prevents it from happening! This pushes people away. Instead, they need to understand and have the faith that, provided they appropriately persist and grow enough they'll have the best chance to reach the objective they so long for, or perhaps something even beyond that.

An example of this would be an aggressive salesperson who follows you around the car lot, not giving you a chance to inspect the vehicles that are there, be with your thoughts, and sort out what you want. He or she hovers over you and practically breathes down your neck, trying to manipulate you into a deal. Most prospective vehicle buyers would want to get away from such an anxious person, and probably never visit that dealership again.

Such people are perceived as desperate, trying to force an outcome which may be premature. A wiser approach is to continue your quest, while letting go of any desire to force it to happen, giving it some time and patience...as you continue to persist and grow. If you go after someone—like a prospect, client, or customer—aggressively, you'll probably chase them away.

Maintain the attitude that you want whatever is best for others, which helps give them a sense of calm assurance. Know deep inside that what's best for them is best for you too. You want them to know that you're somebody they would want to associate with or buy products and services from. You know it will all work out because you keep going no matter what they or any other particular person does. You believe in everyone, but depend on no one... but yourself.

Again, I know how true this is because I've experienced it. In my early 30s, I really wanted to get married and share my life with a wonderful man. I really, really wanted it, so much that I tried to force it to happen. The men I dated apparently sensed my strong attachment to getting married and it probably scared them. That meant that those relationships were, of course, short-lived.

After attending a personal growth seminar, I decided that I would be just fine, no matter how long it took to meet the man who would be the husband I was looking for. Marriage was my desire for sure, but I was not devastated by or putting myself down for being single. I was confident and open-minded, first believing "It could happen" and then that "It will happen." After all, I was continuing to work on myself so I would grow into being my best both personally and professionally, making myself more of the person I needed to be to attract the kind of man I wanted to meet and marry.

Three months later, my husband-to-be walked into my office looking for an ad agency. Instead, he ended up with a wife who loves him very much, and no one was more pleased than me. Shortly after I had let go of my attachment to the outcome, "Mr. Right" appeared!

I'm Fired Up for a Better Life, Principle No. 22—Be Patient

Coupled with the concept of being unattached is patience, which can be challenging when you're working toward an objective. But most dreams require a number of people and things to line up before they can be made to happen. That means having patience and faith as you work through the process. As long as you're consistently taking appropriate action and working on your own personal and professional growth, good things will happen. As Longfellow said…

"The heights that great men reached and kept were not attained by sudden flight. But they, while their companions slept, were toiling upward in the night."

I'm Fired Up for a Better Life, Principle No. 23—Learn from Your Mistakes and Keep Going

Mary Lou Retton, a US Olympic gold medalist in gymnastics who earned a perfect 10, advised…

"Never ever give up on your dreams, and don't be afraid to fail. Failure makes you a stronger person."

Stay Positive with These Suggestions

So how do you use a positive attitude to stay fired up and keep going? Here are a few suggestions:

- *If you have a setback, accept it by saying it's okay, and look for the lesson(s) in it.* Ask yourself, "What can I learn from this experience?" Write out your answer(s).

- *Picture it developing into a positive outcome.* See it with perfect clarity as a victory, with the benefit(s) yet to be realized. One thing leads to another.

- *Be careful how you describe each of your experiences.* Consider so-called failures as learning opportunities. This attitude will help you regard yourself in a positive way—knowing you're not a failure, but rather a student of life, always learning and growing. Be careful about the words you use; words create feelings. Support and encourage yourself. When you catch yourself engaging in negative self-talk, say "Deflect" or "Cancel that." Keep negativity out of your thinking.

- *Ignore failure statistics.* Ignorance of negativity is bliss. When I opened my business, four out of five small businesses failed nationally. If I had known that back then, I might never have started the business. Start taking action and do whatever it takes to make it happen.

- *Avoid negative-thinking people.* They're the ones who are constantly complaining. They whine about everyone and everything—blaming instead of taking responsibility for their difficulties. They're never happy for you when you succeed because they're unhappy. They can't give anyone what they don't have.

- *Seek positive-thinking leaders, mentors, success coaches, and other role models.* Find a leader, mentor, or success coach to counsel with about your business or profession. Associate with people who are more successful than you—people you can learn from and emulate. Duplicate their pattern of success. And keep in mind that you can associate through books, audios, videos, seminars, webinars, and the like; it doesn't always have to be in person.

- *When you face a challenge, keep going.* Again, challenges are for you to *grow through*, not just *go through*. Fill out an action plan and do whatever it takes to keep going.

- *If you're stuck, get out of inertia.* Do something constructive to get yourself moving, as a body in motion tends to stay in motion. Whatever action you take, follow through with it until you finish the assignment you gave yourself. Enjoy the feeling of accomplishment. This might mean meeting new people, calling a new prospect or client, dream-building, or getting together with your leader, mentor, or success coach for support.

  Do *something*, big or small. Take positive action toward improving your life, and it'll help you get back on track.

- *No matter how many situations you have to work through every day, focus on what you can do for others.* Build their dream for a better life, encourage them to be a "good-finder," and help them achieve their objectives. Ask yourself this every day: *"How can I become a more caring person?"* and *"What have I learned that I can share to help others have a more positive attitude?"*

- *Be grateful.* In spite of your challenges, you have much to be thankful for. Without facing challenges and making mistakes, you won't receive the gifts of learning and growing. You're fortunate to have situations to deal with, which is how you learn and grow. As Helen Keller said..."*The best way out is through.*"

I'm Fired Up for a Better Life, Principle No. 24—Cultivate an Attitude of Gratitude

Always honor and appreciate others; it's part of being a caring person. For example, send thank you notes to your leader, mentor, or success coach for their help and support. Maybe a friend or family member babysat for you while you were out growing your business or profession. Do something special for those who help you. If your budget allows, you could send them balloons, a planter, or flowers, in addition to a note. You'll brighten their day and they'll be more likely to want to help you again.

I wanted to thank two local businesspeople in a special way. So I had gourmet gift baskets sent to them. They both said that in all the years they had been in business, no one had ever bothered to thank them with a gift or do anything special for them. They were surprised and delighted.

One of the most valuable ways to maintain a positive attitude, have patience, and stay fired up as you pursue bettering your life is to express gratitude for all your blessings. You'll feel good, too, because *being thankful is one of the main ingredients of being happier and living a better life.*

Be optimistic. Look at challenging situations as opportunities to grow to the next level. Appreciate what you have but focus, with a positive attitude, on where you want to be, instead of the often momentary challenges at hand. Decide to be a happy, joyful person who attracts others like you. No one wants to be around a whiner.

As Eddie Rickenbacker (top-ranking WWI American fighter pilot ace and president of Eastern Airlines) said...

"Think positively and masterfully, with confidence and faith, and life becomes more secure, more fraught with action, riches, in achievement and experience."

Chapter 16

Creating Affirmations to Support Your Dream for a Better Life
Add More Fuel to the Fire

"Affirmations are mental vitamins, providing the supplementary positive thoughts we need to balance the barrage of negative events and thoughts we experience daily."
Tia Walker

You've probably already seen the value of uncovering and replacing myths you might have let stop you in the past. Perhaps you still have some negative beliefs to let go of. One of the best ways to eliminate them is by using affirmations; speak into existence what you want to achieve.

I'm Fired Up for a Better Life, **Principle No. 25—Say Affirmations Daily to Get and Stay Fired Up**

Affirmations are positive present tense statements that people say to themselves daily to help bring about change and increase their self-esteem. Remember how the research mentioned in Chapter 2 showed that people have 40-50,000 thoughts a day, with 75 to 85 percent of them being negative?

Change your internal self-talk so it's all positive in support of your better life. That's where affirmations help. Although experts' opinions vary about the exact number of days, it's generally believed that *any affirmation said consistently every day for 21 to 30 days* will change the programming of the subconscious mind. For particularly deep-seated myths, however, it may require a few months' worth of repeating affirmations. Stick with it and it will impact you. This may seem simplistic, but affirmations work amazingly well. They can help you stay fired up and on track with your action plan.

Even Better Than I Had Hoped

As the owner of an advertising and training company, I've discovered the value of affirmations for business success. Many years ago, I learned that my office manager had the chance to go for her dream of living in Montreal, Canada. So I encouraged her and began searching for a replacement. In addition to placing ads, I created a statement following the guidelines provided later in this chapter. It read "I'm attracting the perfect employee to my business," and I kept repeating it every day while taking a shower. Within two weeks, a young man came to apply for the job.

While discussing his abilities, he casually mentioned that he also had experience as a graphic designer and showed me his portfolio, which was commendable. After interviewing several other applicants, I hired him.

This employee actually took on two jobs: office manager and graphic designer. His arrival also meant that I needed freelance designers less, which saved the company money. Indeed, the perfect employee had shown up—in ways I had never dreamed of. Hiring him got me fired up once more about the power of affirmations!

Letting Go of the Old and Affirming the New

In addition to the above story, I've had quite a number of other great successes with affirmations. As a result of my difficult childhood, I had to deal with some serious challenges. Such situations were a central part of my life, and it was exhausting coping with it all. So I decided to do something about it.

Many years ago I started using affirmations and decided that all experiences, whether positive or negative, were occurring so I could become a more capable person. As a result, today my life is different, and I'm very thankful; I have a wonderful husband, a successful business, great friends, a beautiful, comfortable home, and two frisky, playful cats. I have more peace of mind now than I've ever had. Issues still come up, but I find they're usually small and manageable. Whatever happens, I work through it, learn from it, and move on at an accelerated pace. I'm healthy and my stress level has dropped significantly.

One of the reasons affirmations work so well is that they help re-focus your thinking. Unfortunately, many people tend to focus on the problem rather than the solution, which just creates more of the problem. *You get what you focus on*—focused attention on and taking action toward solutions are keys to peak performance.

Focus on What You Want and *Go for It*

If you're short on cash, concentrate on creating financial secu-rity. Most people just look at their unpaid bills and feel frustrated. If you want more money in your life, develop affirmations which fit your style and meet your needs. For example, "My financial security is increasing as I'm bettering my life." As Earl Nightin-gale, bestselling author of *The Strangest Secret,* said that...

"You are now, and you do become, what you think about."

Think about the better life you want to live, your successes, and your abilities. Focus on what you want, not on what you don't want. Affirmations alone won't bring about any change; you must take action. Former US President Calvin Coolidge put it into per-spective when he said...

"We cannot do everything at once, but we can do something at once."

Sitting at home all day reciting affirmations about being a leader in your business or profession won't make it so. You also need to focus on being a leader by *doing* whatever it takes to make it a reality. Affirming yourself as a successful leader is a dynamic tool that can *assist* you in the process. It will train your mind to see yourself as a leader, while reminding you to do the things neces-sary to bring the idea of being a leader into reality. Affirmations are a great way to reeducate your subconscious about your capacity to succeed and to stay fired up about your life.

Guidelines for Creating Effective Affirmations

Repeating a poorly phrased affirmation can actually do more harm than good. It's the old adage: "Be careful what you ask for; you just might get it." For example, if the affirmation is "I'm finding a 'new car' for very little money," you may be given your family's old clunker, only to find out that the transmission is broken. A better choice would be to say "I'm finding the best, perfectly working, affordable car for me." By being more specific, you enhance your chances of finding the car for you.

Effective Affirmations...

- **Are always phrased in the positive.** When you say, "Don't think about polka dotted giraffes," what immediately comes to mind? Polka dotted giraffes! Focus on what you want—not on what you wish to change. For example, say "I am slim, energetic, and healthy," rather than "I am no longer fat." Eliminate any words that cause you to have a negative picture. If you include the negative idea in your affirmation, you are unintentionally reinforcing what you don't want. You can't focus on the opposite of an idea.

- **Are stated in the present tense** using "I am," and often coupled with action verbs ending in "ing." (e.g. "I am easily finding the ideal prospects and clients for my business.") If someone says they *will be* healthy, that's always in the future—it's not now. You want to start picturing and experiencing the victory today, *right now.*

  Remember, you can only take action when you're living in the present; you can't change the past and you can't live in the future. If there's a quality you want in the future, affirm it in the present—otherwise it will always be out there. For example, say "I'm totally healthy," rather than "I'll be healthy tomorrow." Tomorrow is always in the future and someday typically becomes a new word called never. Make it happen *now!*

- **Are only about you.** Creating affirmations about others doesn't work. A mother may say, for example, "My son is cleaning his room tonight." Her affirmation won't help because it's up to her son to take action. What she could say instead is, "I have a beautiful and orderly house," and ask her son for help. Her affirmation is only effective for the actions *she* takes, which, in this case, is requesting her son's cooperation.

- **Have a visual picture associated with them.** If you say, "I am fired up about my dream," make sure you have a picture in your head of what being fired up looks like. You might envision yourself as excited, listening to your favorite audio, dressed for success, and living your dream life. Or you may sense you're feeling positive and on track, knowing you're fulfilling your true purpose and picturing yourself as confident.

Whatever your affirmation means to you, get a clear vision of it mentally, so you can recognize it when you've achieved it. This is especially important when your affirmation is about a state of mind or something abstract. If you're affirming being a leader in your business or profession, you may want to imagine yourself relaxing with other leaders you know at a resort. Imagine yourself doing something you love to do, like golf, swim, or walk on the beach.

Whatever it is, make sure you can see it in detail. If you want a big, beautiful house, what's it like in your mind? Is it a colonial, a cape, a contemporary, a ranch, a log cabin, or another style? Is it brand new, just a few years old, a lovely older home, or something else? Look through architectural magazines or house plan books and get a crystal clear picture of what you want. Put the details in your affirmation.

- **Have positive emotional components,** such as "I am *easily* and *happily* attracting *ideal* new associates and clients." Adding strong, positive emotion makes the affirmation seem more real to your subconscious. The best affirmations get you fired up about your goal.

  A leader who will be on stage at an upcoming business seminar might say, "I'm excited about easily sharing my story with heart, humility, gratitude, and excitement," to get fired up for the event. I personally like to add "easily" to affirmations because I want it to happen gracefully. Too many make life more difficult than it has to be—why not make it as easy as possible?

- **Are short enough to remember,** since you'll be saying them often. More than about 15 words is usually too much for the mind to easily hold. Recite yours out loud several times for a day or two, until you have it memorized. If you find yourself forgetting the affirmation, you may want to reword it so it's catchy and memorable—like a slogan or jingle.

- **Are to be said every day,** at least once or twice a day, until something positive happens. Some affirmations may take several months or even years to achieve, while others may take effect in just a few weeks. It often depends on your answers to these three questions:

  1) How deeply ingrained was your negative belief which the affirmation is replacing?

  2) Have you let go of the negative belief?

3) Are you stretching toward a huge goal?

Be aware that your affirmations may take more time to take effect than you believe they will, due to those variables. Keep moving toward your dream and be as patient as you can, until you achieve it. Affirmations work only when you *act* on them. As Thomas Henry Huxley said... *"The great end in life is not knowledge but action."*

Record Your Affirmations

Here's a direct and effective method to help you ingrain your affirmations in your conscious and subconscious minds. Talk enthusiastically to yourself into a recorder, even putting your favorite instrumental music on in the background.

For example, say your affirmation is "I'm healthy, wealthy, and wise." Be sure to record it with passion, whatever it may be.

Then do the same with the affirmation in second and third person, i.e., "You, (your name), are healthy and wealthy" and "(Your name) is healthy and wealthy." Do this with all your affirmations. Play your recording in your bathroom, in your vehicle to and from work, or anywhere else where you're not disturbing others or interfering with your job. Always start and end your day on a positive note, as this can quickly help you replace your old programming.

If you prefer not to record your affirmations, just be sure to say them every day for 21 to 31 consecutive days. If you miss a day, start over. Whether you record them or not, post them (which you may want to emphasize with color or stickers) in a place where you'll see them daily.

Affirmations to Help Make Your Dream a Reality

Now, let's use this new information to achieve your dream. Look at the next page, where the Dream Affirmations section appears. There's space for five affirmations. Take a few minutes now to think about the affirmations you could create to support your dream. Make them statements that will assist you in achieving your goals. You are by no means limited to only five—just use five as a starting point.

For someone who is building a business or profession, one affirmation might read, "I am easily meeting and building relationships with the right people." Some other appropriate affirmations may include:

- "I have a clear and powerful vision for my business."
- "I do whatever it takes to achieve my dreams, goals, and objectives."
- "I'm expanding my contact list daily."
- "I'm building a strong team of leaders."
- "I have a strong client (or customer) base."

They are short, emotional, present tense, and provide a visual picture. Using these examples, you are now ready to create affirmations for yourself. Dedicate some time and energy to writing affirmations which will support *your* vision. Remember the guidelines, and have fun with this.

My Dream Affirmations List:

1._____

2._____

3._____

4._____

5._____

The act of creating and writing down your affirmations sends a powerful message to your subconscious—that this is something you really want. You're starting to invest energy into making it happen. Affirmations help you move on from negative thinking patterns and adopt new thoughts and belief systems about yourself. You're taking control, rather than allowing the negative thoughts to affect you. You decide how you think and feel about yourself—you're in charge.

When you're developing affirmations for your dream, you're letting your subconscious know that *you're in charge of your dream,* which is meaningful and worth whatever effort it takes to make it come true. You'll be amazed how the energy in your life relates to your vision, once you commit to it in writing. You'll get fired up and want to work toward making your dream a reality.

Chapter 17
Putting Your Affirmations into Action
Pour More Fuel onto the Fire

*"Life likes to be taken by the lapel and told,
'I'm with you kid. Let's go!'"*
Maya Angelou

The key to using affirmations *effectively* is simple: give yourself *choices*. When you use action options to *choose* how to put your affirmations into action, you place yourself in "the driver's seat," which gets you fired up.

I'm Fired Up for a Better Life, **Principle No. 26—Use Action Options to Get and Stay Fired Up**

Sometimes when a person is endeavoring to help someone resolve a situation, they tell them exactly what to do, giving them no choice. The problem is *this can be felt as a form of control or manipulation*—even if unintentional. With at least three different options on how to take action, people are free to decide for themselves what's best for them. This is essential since so many people have rigidly locked themselves into only one way of doing things.

Certain family structures have systems in place that force children to do things in only one way—the so-called "right way." And while it may have been effective when we were children to follow those standards, it can be severely limiting and frustrating to use them as adults going for what we want.

In order to shift gears and expand our horizons, so we can grow out of our comfort or familiar zones, being flexible is essential.

Through options, we give ourselves permission and the freedom to take appropriate action, while stimulating original thinking which can lead to developing creative solutions. Action options *liberate*.

Creating Your Own Action Options

Now refer to the Dream Affirmations List you completed in the last chapter. Take each of your affirmations and come up with a list of three different action options in support of each one. Hint—*Look at your mind map and you'll find many action options there.*

You're not committing to these actions at this point, unless you want to. You're simply developing some choices as to how you can stay fired up and more effectively make your dream happen. That means you can stretch, grow, and think BIG, harking back to how, as a child, you thought the sky was the limit. Remember, fires burn best when there's lots of fuel.

Could Having More Money and Freedom Be Your Fuel?

It's often necessary to increase your income in order to expand your level of living and make a bigger difference, especially in a way that's near and dear to your heart. For example, if you'd like to ultimately be sharing success ideas with large numbers of people, perhaps around the world, believing it's your mission, you would need the freedom and money to do so. It all depends on what you're aiming to do and how you're choosing to do it.

Unless you have lots of extra money lying around and plenty of time on your hands, you'll have to increase your income and personal freedom in order to fully live your vision. It's an intelligent, practical approach to making what you want happen, and you could be rewarded with deep ongoing satisfaction for having done so.

In my case, in order to afford college while I was a student, I also worked as a telemarketer for a roofing and siding company. Then, to earn extra income while I was still teaching, I worked as a waitress and in as an employee in department stores.

However, without giving up your job, you may choose to build your own home business in order to create another source of income, while growing yourself personally and professionally. As part of your quest for a better life experience, use your action options to make the most effective use of your affirmations, so you can stay fired up to achieve what you want.

The key to staying fired up about your dream for a better life is to keep taking action, no matter how long it takes to achieve it. So stoke up your fire and get moving right now! As you know, time waits for no one.

Chapter 18

Persist Until You Achieve...
Then Keep on Going
Your Fire Burns Best as You Press On

*"Nothing... can take the place of persistence. Talent will
not...Genius will not... Education will not.... Persistence
and determination alone are omnipotent."*
Calvin Coolidge

I'm Fired Up for a Better Life, **Principle No. 27—Finish
What You Start**
This process has five basic phases: 1) Learn about or get an
idea; 2) Understand and accept it; 3) Commit to it; 4) Start
taking action on it; and 5) Do whatever it takes until you achieve
the result you want.

The First Phase is when you learn about or get an idea, which
is where you feel the initial excitement and start getting fired up
about the possibilities of living a better life. You'll most likely be
so excited that you'll want to share your enthusiasm with others.

This is like the beginning part of a romantic relationship. It's
that first phase of contact when everything about the other person
seems perfect, and you can't stop thinking about them; you're ob-
sessed. Some people like the exhilaration of infatuation so much
that they don't stay in relationships long enough, as it would require too much effort to deal with the challenges they would meet
along the way. They quit the relationship before it deepens into a
mature love that would become meaningful and fulfilling. They're

stuck in the first phase, cheating themselves of the great joy that would be experienced over time, believing it can't get any better.

The Second Phase is when you understand and accept the idea, taking possession of it. This is where you sign up to do something, which is good, but won't make you a success. Those who stay stuck in this phase short-change themselves. The great news is anyone can change their thinking and behavior and get unstuck... provided they have a strong enough desire to do so.

The Third Phase starts when you commit. Unfortunately, commitment by itself doesn't make anything happen. If you're excited but your commitment is halfhearted, you can't weather any "storms." For example, when a naysayer is encountered you give up.

The Fourth Phase is when you start taking action, putting effort into supporting your commitment. You're excited as you start following through on what you said you'd do. But you'll never better your life as you would like, missing out on the exhilaration and growth you could have experienced... unless you advance to the final phase.

The Fifth, and Final, Phase is doing whatever it takes for however long it takes to achieve the results you want—essential to improving your life. Keep on persisting as you achieve goals along the way. You'll feel better about yourself and what you've accomplished, and stay fired up to accomplish your next objective.

Finishing Is Essential—*Take Action Until You Succeed, Then Keep Going, Fired Up by a New Objective*

Unfinished objectives detract from the quality of life. How? In many ways, like not finishing books, stopping audios part way through, and not continuing to attend seminars, to the priority "to do" lists that never get completed. This deprives you of the inspiration, education, and incremental accomplishments that can help keep you going and growing.

Not finishing what you start leads to the nasty habit of quitting on yourself and those you care about. Unfinished objectives are a form of self-sabotage which can destroy your self-esteem, and even lead to despair. This is not the way of success.

Every day, we all make commitments or agreements to ourselves or others to do things. Telling your boss you'll be at work on time, setting up lunch with a friend or acquaintance at a certain time and place, or telling your spouse you'll take out the garbage tonight, are all commitments or agreements.

Every time you tell someone you'll do something, you're making a commitment or agreement. Some people call them promises. Most people are pretty good at keeping agreements with others. If they say they'll meet someone at two o'clock, they generally do it.

People who have a reputation of not keeping agreements don't have many friends; they can't be counted on. You probably know people like this, and may have even let them disappoint you. Remember, *broken agreements destroy relationships.*

What about commitments or agreements with yourself? This is where most of us need to focus our awareness and make some changes. Here's an example:

John goes to bed to take a short nap after supper, realizing he hasn't phoned any prospects all week. So he sets his alarm clock for 7 p.m. and tells himself that when he wakes up he'll get on his phone and make calls for an hour.

Instead, after the alarm rings, he grabs the remote and starts watching TV from his easy chair. What has just happened? He let himself down. Once again, he has broken his agreement with himself... and feels miserable. If he does this enough times, he'll no longer believe his own words. His self-esteem slowly diminishes and he may feel tired and anxious. How can this be overcome?

Everything unfinished is a broken agreement and, as long as something is still hanging out there not completed, it saps a little bit of energy. Pile up enough unfinished business and you have a frustrated person who feels like a failure. That's what John may be experiencing, even if he won't admit it. Persistent committed action is rewarded and lack of commitment and inaction leads to stagnancy and failure.

Unfinished business is often linked to procrastination. People who procrastinate may do so for different reasons; from fear of failure to fear of success. Some people are comfortable with chaos, while others feel so overwhelmed that they don't know where to begin. Some believe they work better under pressure, but let it build until it's super stressful. These are just a few of the ways people can limit their capacity to achieve.

Finish what you start. Do what you said you would do. When you've done so, you've kept the agreement. With finishing comes a release of confident energy, a sense that you're a successful, powerfully focused person who gets things done. That energy and attitude can help you achieve your objective. Persist until you achieve what you set out to do, then keep going, fired up for a new objective.

So How Can You Prevent Unfinished Business?

One way to do this is to use a time management system or app. *Write every agreement down,* including those you've made with yourself, and refer to them several times a day. Put a check mark beside or cross out each one as you successfully accomplish it... and feel your confidence grow.

Another approach is to simply say "no." Think carefully before agreeing to do anything. Determine whether you actually want to do it and can do it, considering your priorities. If it doesn't relate to your priorities, don't commit to it.

For example, say your child is on the school soccer team and you've been asked to coach. For one thing, you may not want to do it. Secondly, even if you found the idea appealing, it would require a lot of evening and weekend hours. This may cut into the time needed to get ahead in your business or profession.

Therefore, you could reply, "I appreciate the confidence you have in me, but I already have a very busy schedule with a lot of commitments. No, I'm not the person to do it. Have you considered asking George or Harry?"

A third way, as discussed earlier, is to *renegotiate the agreement.* Rather than breaking an agreement, be clear that you are renegotiating it. You're making a mutually acceptable change or compromise. This enables you to maintain your integrity and self-esteem, and it creates trust and respect with your friends, loved ones, and others with whom you associate.

Clean Up Your Home Environment—*De-Junk*

Another powerful way to eliminate unfinished business and get your energy fired up is to *look at how you live and physically take action.* To resolve the unfinished status of half-read books, develop a plan to complete them, provided they relate to your priorities. Recycle papers, bottles, jars, and cans.

Clean out your closets to at least de-clutter them, and make room for new clothes when the time comes. Take any old clothes you and your family no longer wears to a friend in need, the Red Cross, Goodwill, Volunteers of America, Salvation Army, a church, a shelter for the homeless, or another charity in the country where you live. Throw out any outdated cans of food or half-eaten boxes of stale crackers.

Clean up your living environment and eliminate any other clutter. Walk around your home to see which areas always catch your eye because they're messy. Most people have at least a couple of areas that need tidied up. Resolve to take action, one step at a time, and organize them. Eliminate all the things you aren't using and either sell or give them away to a charity, or to someone else who can use them. In other words—*de-junk*. Remember, one person's junk is another's treasure.

Some nonprofit organizations will even come to your home and pick up all useable items that you no longer need, want, or use. This is a powerful and positive exercise. One woman cleaned out all of her closets. The next week, as a surprise, her husband gave her three new dresses. She had made room for the new clothes by getting rid of the old ones.

Making Agreements Toward Living a Better Life

Now let's return to your quest for a better life, which you say you want. Go to your List of Affirmations with your action options from Chapter 17 and your Action Worksheet. You've listed at least 15 different actions you could take to better your life.

Now recall the **Third Phase—Commitment**—where you're making an agreement with yourself, and possibly others, to take action on something. Write out the specific action option you're choosing to do, your target date for when the action is to be completed.

For example, a man wanted a significant sum of money for a wildlife project. One of his affirmations was about gaining financial independence through his own business. He had given himself three action options as to how to do that. So he chose the one he wanted to do and made a time commitment.

He accomplished the first action option step by the date he had set, and actually completed the second step earlier than the date he had set. His next step was to list all the other action steps he wanted to take, along with their target dates.

Now it's time for you to take more action on your objective. Choose your action option and make your action steps *small, clear, and realistic*. For example, it's wiser to have an action step like:

"Go to the home show and meet five new positive people," rather than just "Meet some people." The more specifically and clearly you describe each step, the more likely you are to accomplish them.

Review your action options and set some optimistic goals. For example, schedule ten appointments for your business or profession in a given week. If you get cancellations or no shows, you can still meet your goal of five activities that week. Before you set your goal, be sure to think of how you'll reward yourself when you achieve it.

It's important not to work just for the sake of working. Give yourself incentive to keep going by knowing ahead of time how you're going to celebrate your accomplishment. For example, after you've met your goals every week for a month, if it's in your budget you could take your spouse or family out for a Saturday or Sunday breakfast or brunch.

Finally, after you've made your list of action steps with target dates, see yourself as successful. Remember that the top professional athletes in baseball, basketball, football, tennis, golf, soccer, and other sports first visualize their success; they see themselves winning. They get fired up. Every play, every swing, every movement is seen perfectly and clearly. Then when they're actually engaged in playing the sport, they're much more likely to do so with excellence.

Some of them, like Tara Cross Battle, who was a member of the US Women's Olympic Volleyball team, used music to inspire and motivate themselves. She listened to gospel music before games. "It gets me fired up and ready to go!" she exclaimed.

Take a few minutes and put on some inspiring, soul stirring music. See yourself fired up and successfully taking action and completing the task by your target date, on every one of the steps you listed. Allow yourself to experience it fully. Feel all the positive emotions and energy; hear the cooperative comments from the mentor, leader, or success coach you've asked for help. *Picture ease and success every step of the way.* See yourself succeeding, and you're on your way. No matter how long it takes to accomplish your objectives, you know you can do it.

In the sage advice of Earl Nightingale...

"Never give up on a dream just because of the time it will take to accomplish it. The time will pass anyway."

Chapter 19

Paint Your Picture of Success
Vigorously Stoke Your Fire

*"Keep your dreams alive. To achieve anything requires faith
and belief in yourself, vision, hard work, determination, and
dedication. All things are possible for those who believe."*
Gail Devers

Here's a great way to picture your dream for living a better life, and make it come more alive in your mind and heart. You're now ready to use your vision of the future you yearn for by creating a powerful tool—a dream collage—to help you make it your new reality.

I'm Fired Up for a Better Life, Principle No. 28—Create a Dream Collage

A dream collage, or treasure map as some call it, is a visual representation of your successfully realized dream. It's a terrific way to stay fired up about it. Starting with a white or crème-colored poster board or foam core, paste up pictures and words that represent the elements of your currently envisioned dream for a better life on this board.

You can create these images, cut them from magazines and newspapers, or use photographs you have taken. A combination of all these things would be even better. One of the most important elements of your collage is that your picture is on it—put yourself in the dream to make it seem more real and personal.

I'm Fired Up for a Better Life, Principle No. 29—Let the Child Inside Your Heart Come Out and Play

Have you ever been to an amusement park and watched the adults? You'll notice many adults there without children; yet they're laughing and playing anyway. One of the reasons Disney World is so successful is that adults can "let their hair down" and be kids again.

Inside each of our hearts is a spontaneous, happy child. Some people are good at inviting this fun-loving child to come out and play, while others keep them locked away. It's essential that you invite the child inside your heart to participate in your dream. That child is quite creative, knows no boundaries, and thinks only in terms of possibilities. You can benefit by connecting with and accessing these gifts. This is especially true when you're creating your collage.

Lisa wanted to build her business and have a happy marriage. Within a year of creating her dream collage, she was happily married to her new husband and sharing her successful business with him. She has experienced more joy than ever, and continues to grow and improve her life.

Lisa actually created a separate collage for her finances, health, family, business, and such. Placing them strategically around her home, almost everywhere she looks there's a collage to help keep her focused and fired up about her goals.

Making My Dreams a Reality with the Help of a Collage

I've personally had tremendous results with dream collages, finding them to be powerful and effective. Many years ago I created one focused mainly on my personal life. I wasn't married yet and, as mentioned before, wanted to find a great husband. So I picked out key words to get me fired up like "The Best Man Ever." I cut out a picture of a wedding dress I liked, along with pictures of places I wanted to visit with my new husband.

In the upper left hand corner, I put a picture of myself with words from a magazine that said "Her Brilliant Career," "High Profile Creativity" and "Woman to Watch." These phrases kept the flame alive inside of me and inspired me to achieve. There were also photos of sailboats, since sailing is my favorite hobby, plus other meaningful words and pictures.

To help improve your life, here are some ideas of what you could do to create your own dream collage. First, put a picture of yourself and your spouse or family in the center, including the level, position, or title you want to achieve in your business or profession under the photo. If you enjoy traveling, get some brochures from a travel agent or online with pictures of your favorite places, putting the name of the location below the photo. Include pictures of sports you like such as golfing, hot air ballooning, sailing, flying, deep-sea fishing, and so forth. If you want a new boat, airplane, or something else, include them as well.

Add pictures of your dream home, jewelry, vehicles(s), motorhome, or anything else you may want. Also be sure to include intangible dreams like "healthy and wealthy," "debt-free," "financially secure," and "time with family." Include what suits you and have fun with it.

After your collage is completed, take a photo of it. Print out some enlargements to put up around the house, as well as some smaller photos for your wallet and vehicles. You could even make a screen saver out of it. See your dreams in front of you as often as possible. This will help keep you motivated by reminding you what you're striving for.

Without exception, *everything on my collage became a reality!* I even married "The Best Man Ever" in a dress similar to the one on my collage, which I designed and had custom made. We also went to the Caribbean for our honeymoon and have since chartered large sailboats there.

The most surprising thing about the collage was something I never would have predicted. That little upper left-hand corner for and about my career, "High Profile Creativity," came true in remarkable ways. I was honored to receive a national award from the Small Business Administration for my work in helping to create a non-profit organization to help women start and stay in business.

That award resulted in my flying to Washington, DC, and attending a ceremony in the Rose Garden at the White House, with then-President Bush. Seven of us were then honored at a Congressional luncheon with over 700 people, which led to exposure in some national magazines.

For years now, my husband, Spencer, and I have had a couple's dream collage based on our life together, which we continue to update.

It covers every aspect from romance and travel, as well as our spiritual life and financial goals. It's about five feet long and resides in our bedroom. We look at it regularly for inspiration and to keep on track.

Now It's Your Turn!

Schedule an entire morning, afternoon, or evening for this activity, as it can make a big difference in your ability to focus on your dream for a better life. It's fun, engrossing, and well worth the time put into it. You'll be amazed at how real your dream becomes and how fired up you'll get looking at it displayed on your collage. Here's all you need to get started:

- A large piece of poster board or foamcore.
- Tape or glue, and a pair of scissors.
- Magazines with the topics that reflect your dream.
- Construction paper and markers to make words and sketch pictures.
- A photo of yourself and your spouse or family.
- Photos and pictures of various material things you aspire to own, goals you want to accomplish, and objectives you want to achieve.
- Your imagination.

Where Do You Get Your Ideas?

Focus on your better life description and action plan for now, for one year, for three years, and for five years from now. Imagine you're painting a picture of your success that fully portrays all you want to create and how you want to live. Look for pictures and words in magazines and cut out everything that appeals to you. You can also use photographs.

Take your time and make sure what you want is completely represented. If you need additional money for your dream, draw a pot of gold at the end of a rainbow, with the amount of money you believe you need to live a better life.

Also be sure to put the words "I'm living a better life" on your collage to help you believe and affirm that you can achieve your desired life. And definitely *include a picture of yourself, and your spouse or family* in the collage, as this is essential to your ability to see yourself as fully successful, living a more meaningful life, making a bigger difference, and affecting others in a more positive way.

Once you have all the pieces of your collage, including the words, photos, and graphics you want, as well as a photo of yourself and your spouse or family, review them to be sure every item clearly communicates what you want. *Be specific.* For example, write a fake check to yourself for, say, $1,000,000, and put it on the collage. The more you see it, the more familiar and comfortable you become with the idea of having it.

Make your collage colorful, so the elements of your dream come alive when you look at it. Test each picture emotionally—does it get you fired up or not? If not, leave it off the collage. A good way to determine this is if you get goose bumps or smile, or have some other positive reaction. This indicates the picture has meaning and value for you. When you're happy with all the pieces of the collage, lay them out on the board, which is preferably white or crème colored. Play with the layout and move things around until everything looks just right, and then tape or glue them down.

Once the glue has dried, put your collage where you'll see it every day. A good location could be the refrigerator door, or on a bedroom wall. Look at it daily—*notice how you're doing and give yourself credit for your successes.* Let it get you fired up and help you move closer and closer toward living a better life.

A Life-Long Dream Come True

Sally's forever dream was to go to Africa and study wildlife. Never one to quit, as a college student she persisted in discovering ways to make it a reality. First, she created a large dream collage which she hung on her bulletin board. She covered it with pictures of Africa, a *National Geographic* map, and a photograph from a camera catalog focused on a wild heron, with a notepad and pencil nearby. It expressed completely what she wanted to be doing—studying wildlife. Sally studied her collage daily, visualized living the dream, and took consistent action toward achieving it.

That fall at school, she met with a wildlife writer to find out how she could do research in Africa. This led her to connect with a professor who had just received a study grant for Tanzania.

During the school year, Sally scrambled to create the resources she thought she would need to go to Africa; depleting her savings, she had to rush through her final class work so she could make the trip. Following her vision, she took a leap of faith and booked three different sets of flight reservations for Tanzania, not knowing when the expedition would be leaving or if she would even be a part of it. Finally, she got confirmation of the departure date, and that she would be conducting research on hippopotamus communication.

Alone but completely fired up, this courageous young woman traveled across the ocean to Tanzania, "the most foreign place" she had ever experienced. Nearly missing her connection with the safari, she joined the expedition and headed for the bush. There she spent her days observing two groups of hippos and their interactions with each other. She fondly remembers that first night happily thinking, "I'm living my dream. This is wonderful and it's real." Sally had never felt more confident or fulfilled in her life.

Many adventures challenged her courage and thinking abilities during her time in Africa. For example, she got stranded overnight on a local bus and was criticized by negative-thinking people because she was traveling alone. But she triumphed over the difficulties and ended up spending four exciting months in Tanzania, Kenya, and Zimbabwe.

The fact that she had succeeded in making her dream come true gave her a reserve of confidence and courage which she needed when she got home. Shortly after her return, she came face to face with some serious family difficulties. But the act of achieving her dream, of having her collage become reality so perfectly, served to spur her on and keep her going... no matter what challenges she and her family faced.

As she said later, "Once you've made a dream come true, you know you can do it again. It's just a matter of choosing what dream to work on. I know I can do anything now." Sally's courage and success have inspired her to persist in further endeavors, firing up others to do the same.

You Now Have a Powerful and Exciting Tool
Show your collage only to positive-thinking people who you feel will not only appreciate your dream, but also believe in and encourage you. Otherwise, it's best to keep it to yourself. Congratulations on your work so far. You've made a terrific tool for staying fired up, as you work toward your better life dream.

Chapter 20
Avoid Dream-Delaying Hooks
Make Any Smoldering Embers Catch Fire

*"Whether you think you can or you
think you can't, you're right!"*
Henry Ford

I'm *Fired Up for a Better Life*, **Principle No. 30—Avoid the Hooks.** In the old vaudeville acts where a performer was all fired up singing or dancing, a giant hook would come out and pull the person offstage in mid-act.

In real life, they're the hooks, or obstacles, that can take you out of the "act" of pursuing your dream. They can douse the flames of your enthusiasm and discourage you from working toward a better life, but *only* if you let them. Knowing about these hooks ahead of time can help you be on the alert, so you can prevent them from delaying or stopping you.

While people's dreams vary, many sincerely want to directly touch others' lives in a positive way. Since they want to connect with those who could benefit from what they have to offer, they simply can't afford to get snagged by any dream-delaying hooks.

A Wake-Up Call—Is This All There Is?

Sam and Virginia had been married for ten years, had two wonderful kids, and appeared to be happy and successful. But one day after the kids were in bed, Virginia cried out, "Sam is this all there is? I don't think I can take it anymore. It seems like all we're doing is working, barely paying the bills, trying to squeeze a life out of it all, but it's getting old. Sure, we have a nice house and vehicles, but it feels like we're never going to get out of debt, save for the kids' college, or even have a decent retirement. We'll probably have to work 'till we drop. When are we ever going to get beyond this boring routine and live a better life? It's getting to be a real drag, and we've just got to do something about it."

Sam nodded in agreement, giving Virginia a big hug, assuring her, "Somehow we'll find a way."

Incredibly, later that week they were visiting Sam's brother, Ed, and his wife Gloria, who lived an hour away. At dinner, they shared their "Is this all there is?" conversation, not aware that Ed and Gloria had their own business and could help them.

After the couple left, Ed and Gloria realized they had never shared their business with them as they had erroneously assumed everything was going well for them. The following week, Ed called Sam and asked if he and Gloria were serious about wanting to make some changes in their lives. Sam adamantly said, "Yes!" and they set up a time for both couples to get together.

It was a gratifying experience to see how Sam and Virginia regained the hope they once had for a better life. Ed and Gloria felt like they were making a positive difference. The great bonus was that they all became closer as a family as they proceeded to build their businesses together, with even the kids happily participating.

This example has people as key components on the giving and receiving ends. They help other people in order for their own better lives to be fully realized.

Dream-Delaying Hook No. 1—*Attachment to a Particular Outcome.* What if Sam and Virginia had refused the opportunity? Being committed to their business, Ed and Gloria wouldn't have taken it personally. They would have kindly respected Sam and Virginia's decision, preserving the relationship, leaving the door open for a potential change of interest later on. This could be referred to as "High Commitment, No Attachment." Forcing the issue would only have alienated Sam and Virginia.

Ed and Gloria understood rejection is part of success and many people make excuses, excusing themselves from creating the better life they say they want. To their own detriment, far too many people complain about their life situation, but won't do anything to change it!

When you're working on a dream that involves others in its attainment, maintain the philosophy of "for the benefit of all concerned." That way there's no dream-delaying hook here, and you can give your best without being attached to the outcome.

You diligently invest yourself in your quest, but aren't thwarted if certain outcomes along the way aren't realized. You're fired up, committed to your goals, whatever it takes, while being concerned about what's best for everyone involved. What's best for them is best for you! Maintain determination; persist until you make your dream a reality, then keep on persisting for the next one.

How can this be done? The key is to have targeted measurable results, which enable you to see that the work you're doing is helping others. Realize that if your efforts touch even one person you've made a difference. Feel good about that. Make your daily success list, acknowledging the "baby" steps and tiny changes, as well as the big achievements. Over time, small accomplishments add up to significant improvements; they're part of the process.

Dream-Delaying Hook No. 2—*Believing Other People's Responses and Behaviors Are About You.* I used to think I was the cause of how others behaved and responded toward me. Once I got it that other people say and do certain things because of what's going on in *their* lives, I gained the freedom to just be myself and not let them upset me. No one can ruin your day without your permission!

If you let what others say or don't say, or do or don't do, affect your attitude about yourself and what you're doing, you're in for an emotional rollercoaster ride. The response to sharing what you have to offer can never be guaranteed. If you let someone's negative response or behavior get to you, you could internalize it and reject yourself, creating doubt about what you're doing in striving for a better life, sending yourself into a tailspin. You could also ruin the relationship, resulting in them never wanting to associate with you.

Prospective clients or associates say no because of their attitudes and/or life situations. For example, they may have expressed interest in what you shared, but their spouse may have rejected it. When you're sharing or reaching out to others, don't take on their emotional reactions or rejections as personal affronts. Stay focused on where you're going and continue to feel good about what you're doing—*regardless of how others may respond or behave.*

For example, the boss may *not* be yelling because he's unhappy with your performance; he may have had an argument with his wife and was inappropriately venting his anger on innocent you. The child in the cancer wing who won't smile at a volunteer's funny stories may be too sick from chemotherapy to notice anything else. The homeless person who received the coat someone donated may not say, "thank you" because of his or her shame about being homeless.

Dream-Delaying Hook No. 3—*Quitting.* When you have a dream, it will take time and effort to achieve it. Building a business or profession, making a better life, writing a book, or creating a program for children are examples of long-term dreams. Unfortunately, people often quit just short of making the breakthrough that would have enabled them to achieve their objective.

Remember when we talked about finishing what you start and how many people never do? They rob themselves of the satisfaction and burst of energy that comes from completion. Sometimes they quit because they're impatient or are limited by a lack of vision. As Winston Churchill said, *"Never, never, never give in...."*

Dream-Delaying Hook No. 4—*Overlooking Small Victories.* While reaching objectives generally takes longer than what we anticipate, it's important to know we're making progress, no matter how small. Many expect instant gratification, for example: take this pill and you'll feel great; and buy now, pay later. Ads suggest weight loss can be instant and permanent with a certain product. Commercials imply driving a certain vehicle will give you the freedom and excitement you yearn for, as well as getting cash back.

The truth is bringing a worthwhile dream to fruition takes time, relentless pursuit, and requires an unknown number of actions in overcoming obstacles. Keep in mind that *success is a life-long journey, a progression—it's not a once and done deal.* So keep doing whatever it takes and enjoy the process as much as possible.

Recognizing daily successes will help keep you fired up and motivated; you'll know you're on your way. If, for example, a physical therapist felt like a failure because her patient with a broken leg wasn't able to walk normally in one day, she'd be missing the big picture. Dreams take time to realize, requiring consistent long-term action. Recognizing progress along the way is essential; it's a key piece for staying fired up to finish what you start.

Chapter 21

Stay Fired Up to Go and Grow
Keep Building Your Fire Bigger and Bigger

*"The real secret of success is enthusiasm...excitement.
When [people] get excited, they make a success of their
lives. You can do anything if you have enthusiasm."*
Walter Chrysler

Being positive and staying fired up while pursuing your aspirations is an ongoing process, requiring conscious awareness and effort. Monitoring your progress is valuable, but knowing what keeps your fire burning and energizes you is even more valuable.

All of us have had negative experiences. If you miss a good opportunity, get hurt physically or emotionally, are criticized or rejected, you may tend to respond negatively. The natural human reaction is to turn inward and lick your wounds. However, there's a much more effective way of dealing with negativity. Shift into a positive attitude—*look for the lesson in the negative experience and grow from it.*

This story demonstrates the point. To most people, witnessing war-torn Bosnia would have been negative. Seeing all the people who suffered and the orphaned children would have melted almost anyone's heart—like it did Gerry McClure's. She and her mother visited Bosnia for two weeks, supplying badly needed medical supplies to a refugee center. Gerry was deeply affected by the children's pain. When she returned, her father's diagnosis of terminal cancer further shook her. She knew she needed to do something to make a difference, and created a sense of urgency for herself.

Inspiration came to her one night in a life-changing dream, leading to the birth of a new business specifically designed to benefit children. Financially prepared, she left her position as VP for an international banking firm on Wall Street to do something she felt would provide a more meaningful, fulfilling life. Founding Heaven on Earth, Inc., which manufactured several different multiracial non-denominational dolls meant to represent guardian angels, she donated at least 10 percent of its pre-tax profits to charities worldwide.

Every "Angel Gram" doll's tag was imprinted with the words: *"This angel comes to you from above with the message of joy and God's love."* The dolls were available in black, white, Hispanic, and Asian; each one also had an audio of the song, "Your Angel's Always There," an angel pendant for the child to wear, a *Little Book of Angels,* and a map showing where the donations from Heaven on Earth have gone around the world.

With six employees and revenues of over $2 million in today's dollars, the business donated money and supplies to the Croatian Emergency Relief Fund, the Children's Welfare Institute in China, and the International God-Parenthood to Bosnian Children Organization, among others. Gerry's challenging negative experiences led to her realizing that she wanted to share love and give a sense of hope to others. As Gerry said...

"Make a promise to do one GREAT thing in your lifetime.... If you want to be surrounded by blessings in your life, learn to pass the blessing first."

What's Negative and Positive for *You*?

As you work on improving your life, identify which activities are negative and which are positive for you. This will help you be more aware and stay pointed in the direction you want to go. Spending more time in a positive state will enable you to think bigger, do more, and create better results. It keeps your fire blazing brightly, while serving as a beacon to others.

Positive actions are those which help you feel better about yourself, stronger, more successful, and more competent. For some people, a positive action might be seeing an uplifting movie, giving a hug, reading an inspiring book, or going to a motivating seminar. For others, it might mean doing something they've never done before... just for the fun of it, to keep themselves fired up.

These are in sharp contrast to the negative activities that cause people to shut down, feel small, weak, tight, depressed, de-energized, inadequate, and disempowered. Watching violent TV shows or movies, playing violent video games, viewing or listening to the negative news, or complaining about things or criticizing others all tend to put people in a disturbed or negative state of mind. This de-energizes them, taking them off track from pursuing their dream.

Choose Positive Activities

Knowing what is positive and negative for you assists you in making conscious shifts in behavior and attitude. You'll purposely seek positive activities, especially if you're tired or depressed. People who are the most effective in achieving their aspirations stay fired up by regularly participating in positive, uplifting activities, while avoiding negative attitudes and behaviors, or transforming them into positive ones. They also avoid negative-thinking people, are optimistic, and always look for the good.

Consciously choosing to attend a motivational seminar is an example of how this awareness works. If, instead, you stay at home and watch TV, which often promotes and feeds into negative thinking, you're likely to feel even less motivated than when you turned it on!

On the other hand, when you associate with positive people who are going somewhere, you feel good about yourself and get reinforced that you can accomplish something. While spending time with upbeat, supportive friends and role models benefits you, visiting with co-workers, family, and friends who are whiners rather than winners only wears you down. These are all choices you make regularly, that either help or hinder you in moving forward.

Here's a way to help you determine what's positive or negative for you. A series of activities is listed with a blank next to each one. Rest assured that there are no right or wrong answers; there's only information. The same action may be positive to some, yet negative to others. It just depends on what you like to do.

Positive or Negative Activities—*An Exercise*

Put a P in the blank for Positive if it lifts your spirits when you do it, or an N if this activity is Negative and brings you down.

_____	Exercising	_____	Attending a seminar
_____	Being under pressure	_____	Dancing
_____	Rushing somewhere	_____	Jogging
_____	Meeting new people	_____	Paying bills
_____	Sailing	_____	Hugging
_____	Napping	_____	Honoring your spouse
_____	Doing paperwork	_____	Budgeting
_____	Going to work	_____	Being indoors
_____	Being in nature	_____	Playing with children
_____	Watching funny movies	_____	Emailing and texting
_____	Taking a hot bath	_____	Singing
_____	Swimming	_____	Listening to music
_____	Traveling	_____	Arguing
_____	Smiling	_____	Watching the news
_____	Grocery shopping	_____	Cooking
_____	Doing the laundry	_____	Painting/drawing
_____	Starting a new project	_____	Completing a project
_____	Going to church	_____	Helping others
_____	Reaching goals	_____	Sharing successes
_____	Cleaning out closets	_____	Dream-building
_____	Seeing friends	_____	Crying
_____	Flying	_____	Reading a book
_____	Walking	_____	Speaking to a group
_____	Phoning people	_____	Using social media
_____	Surfing the Internet	_____	Time with family
_____	Gardening	_____	Hobby activities

Did completing the list help you to better understand yourself? Some people love doing laundry because it's therapeutic and they feel good about providing fresh, clean clothes for their family. They focus on the prize. Others view it as a chore—they focus on the price. Some dread meeting new people, but those moving on look forward to it with keen anticipation; they're excited about expanding their network of friends and acquaintances who could then become customers, clients, and associates.

You may have also found that your answers would have been different had you imagined other specifics about the category. For example, seeing certain friends might be a positive, while seeing other friends might be a negative.

There are moments when paperwork can be really satisfying, but other times when it simply stacks up, perhaps causing you to feel overwhelmed. All that matters here is that you *learn what works for you*. Highlight all the P (Positive) activities in your favorite color and keep the list for reference. Be sure to add other activities that are positive for you that aren't on the list. Depending on your priorities, it may not be the time to do some of these things. But you'll find that just thinking about them can get you fired up.

Any time you find yourself getting negative, learn from the experience and deliberately look for the good as you do or think about something positive. Beyond that, plan your day around the kinds of experiences you would like to have—those that stir your sparks, set you on fire, and move you closer to what you want. No matter what you do, though, *focus on the prize* not the price.

For me, some of my most positive experiences have involved travel and exploration. I studied a little art and sculpture in prep school (my mother had been an artist) and was looking forward to seeing the work of Michelangelo in Florence, Italy. But no one could have prepared me for my reaction to Michelangelo's David.

Not sure where it was in the museum, I flipped through my guidebook, wandering from room to room until I entered the hall where David was showcased. It was so spectacular that I burst into tears. I didn't expect to react to it like that, but I was moved by its magnificence. Michelangelo said that he had simply cut away all the rock that wasn't a part of David!

Years later, I had a similar experience in Paris where the impressionist paintings of Renoir and Monet were housed in a quaint museum called Le Jeu du Pomme. After I climbed the stairs and came face to face with Monet's sailing paintings, again, I started crying, deeply moved by the beauty and brilliance of what I saw. These positive activities are now treasured memories that fire me up whenever I think about them.

You may have had moments like these too. Choose your activities wisely, with the intention of staying open-minded and positive, and you're much more likely to keep moving forward. You're more fired up and optimistic about achieving your dreams, goals, and objectives, and feel energized in striving for them, full of anticipation. Your fire can be stoked at every level, and your blaze can burn brighter and brighter, as you go and grow.

Chapter 22

27 Tips for Staying
Fired Up for a Better Life
Make Your Fire Burn Brighter and Brighter

*"Into each life comes a time to grow when dreams
must be spoken and wings must be tried...so reach for
your dreams, spread your new wings, and fly."*
Florence Littauer

I'm *Fired Up for a Better Life*, **Principle No. 31—Do What Winners Do to Stay Fired Up.** You've read stories about famous athletes and heroes who kept going no matter what. They stayed fired up and achieved their dreams. Even those skilled in personal development have times when it's challenging to stay motivated, and that's what this chapter helps you do. It's chock full of tips to help you get fired up and stay fired up. Use them regularly, especially when you get stuck. If one doesn't do it for you, use another until you get going again. Then keep moving, showering sparks on your fire to keep it blazing away.

Count Your Blessings First

Before you start reviewing the 27 Tips for Staying Fired Up, *consider your many blessings, write them down, and be grateful for them.* No matter what your circumstances may be, there are always positive aspects to life, as illustrated by the following story.

When Becky Ferry was a teenager she knew what it took to be a champion. She cared for Jersey cows on the family farm, many of which were blue ribbon winners. What's extraordinary is not that the cows were winners or even that Becky took great pleasure in their victories. What's noteworthy is Becky's winning attitude after all the tragedy she had faced in her young life.

When she was nine, Becky's coat got caught on the spinning shaft of a machine that unloads corn from a wagon. Before anyone could stop the machine, she suffered multiple fractures of both her knees and legs. The only safe medical solution was amputation.

Incredibly, the first thing Becky asked when she came out of surgery was, "Will I be able to show cows again?" Her enthusiasm and fired up attitude carried her a long way... through grueling months of rehabilitation and physical therapy. While fitted with prosthetics, she found them unwieldy for work on the farm. When working with her beloved cows, she preferred to wear her "stubbies"—short wide rubber platforms which give her stability and balance but not height.

In spite of her physical disability, she maintained a "B" average at school, even though she worked with the cows ten hours a day. She also learned to swim again, and always looked forward to a future filled with promise, including raising heifers. Her favorite cow, Sunny, a honey-colored Jersey, earned the coveted Farmer's Museum Dairy Cup, which Becky accepted with great joy, as she was truly thankful and fired up. That's her fundamental outlook on life and it keeps her going every day. We could all learn a great deal from Becky's fired up attitude.

Remember These Two Examples

Wilma Rudolph, the first woman runner to win three gold medals at a single Olympic event, overcame severe physical disabilities to become an athlete. At four, she was struck with double pneumonia and scarlet fever, losing the use of her left leg. Her family had a fired-up attitude, though, and began massaging her leg four times a day. By age 11 she was able to run normally, and by high school she was an outstanding athlete. As a black Southern woman in the US, her challenges were many. But she beat them all to triumph at the Olympics and was named to the Women's Sports Hall of Fame.

Ski instructor Pete Seibert was called crazy when he told others about his vision. From age 12 on, he had the dream of building a top-level ski resort in Colorado. Without any money, but with lots of vision and focus, he got others fired up for his dream. Out of a sheep pasture, Pete went on to create and develop one of the most famous resorts in the US—Vail, Colorado. To say the least, he created and lived a better life.

27 Tips for Staying Fired Up for a Better Life

The next few pages include detailed explanations for every tip. For your future use, there's an easy-to-read list of all 27 at the end of the book. They're tried and true ways to stay fired up. Find the ones that appeal to you the most, while not interfering with your priorities. Perhaps you'll even discover some new ones.

Do whatever it takes to keep yourself fired up. Be a good example and keep moving and growing. *Get fired up, stay fired up, and live a better life while empowering others to do the same.*

Staying Fired Up for a Better Life, Tip No. 1—*Identify What You Truly Want in Your Life.* Periodically update the list of what you desire (Chapter 3) as it can change faster than you realize. What was once important can give way to something new; one thing leads to another. College majors are good examples. Many students pick a major as a freshman, only to switch to another as a junior. Furthermore, most grads don't end up working in a field related to what they majored in, which may well be true for you.

Either way, your job or career may have developed into something different than what you thought it would be, and may want to substantially change your life's work or be able to retire from it early. Perhaps you're building a secondary income outside of your work so, at some point, you won't need a job anymore.

Remember where you listed the circumstances in your life which you didn't want (Chapter 3)? Periodically make a new list to see where you are with that. It'll help you clarify what you truly value and want... and get you fired up about doing whatever it takes to achieve it.

Staying Fired Up for a Better Life, Tip No. 2—*Dream-Build Regularly.* Dream-build as often as you can. It makes the accomplishment of your dream seem more believable; you start taking "ownership" of it. Test drive your dream car. Tour houses you'd like to live in. Go to car shows, boat shows, air shows, hobby shows, and the like. Take pictures of everything you want in your life and have someone else take photos of you with them. Stay in touch with the various elements of your dream and meet other dreamers too.

Some of the greatest relationships you'll ever build can begin at those places, with people who have something in common with you. This makes it easier for you to build bridges to new relationships. Dream-build regularly to keep yourself fired up about where you're going. These activities are fun and free or inexpensive, don't take much time, and can be key ways for you to expand the number of people you know—a prime ingredient for success in any field.

Staying Fired Up for a Better Life, Tip No. 3—*Keep Agreements with Yourself and Others.* Agreements are described throughout this book. Remember, every commitment you make to yourself and others is an agreement. Every time you break an agreement, you sabotage a relationship (which could be with yourself!), your success, and your self-esteem. If you find your life just isn't working as you would like—*take a look at your agreements.* Fulfill them or renegotiate them. Write them down; and when you make an agreement be sure to keep it.

Staying Fired Up for a Better Life, Tip No. 4—*Update Your Dream Collage and Regularly Picture Yourself Living the Life You Want.* Your dream collage is a dynamic tool for seeing your dream for a better life as a reality. To many, seeing is believing. Look at your collage daily to help you believe through seeing. Update it regularly with new pictures, words, and symbols as you achieve various aspects of your vision for a better life. Either modify your collage or replace it as needed. Keep it fresh and exciting.

Clearly picture yourself living that better life you so dearly would love to live. Every time you do, it's likely you'll experience something special and some new aspect of your desired life will appear. The more clearly you envision it—*the sooner you're likely to be living it.*

Staying Fired Up for a Better Life, Tip No. 5—*Review Your Daily Success Lists.* This will really help you to remind yourself that you've already achieved various successes. You'll recognize how much you've already done and *have* accomplished, and that you can do so again, and again, and again.

Whenever I feel like I'm not getting anywhere on my current dream, I review my daily success lists. My whole attitude then shifts and I get fired up by reflecting on all that I've already done; I see myself as a successful achiever. It boosts my confidence and gets me fired up *again* about achieving my new desire and doing whatever's necessary to make it come to pass, getting me out of any inertia that was bogging me down. Reviewing your daily success lists can get you fired up again and moving as well.

Staying Fired Up for a Better Life, Tip No. 6—*Create a Feel Good Folder and View It Often.* A "Feel Good Folder" is a great tool to help you overcome disappointments, get inspired, and stay fired up, making it invaluable in supporting you in achieving your objectives. You could keep it in your planning or time/activity management system or app. Some people also keep a paper file folder, brightly colored or covered in exciting wrapping paper.

Include photos of and messages and greeting cards from your loved ones and other favorite people. Also include photos of places and activities, daily success lists, pets, animals, copies of some of the forms you've completed in this book, pictures of vacation spots you'd like to visit, vehicles that really touch your heart, and other things that are meaningful to you. They could also be items such as thank you notes, special letters, cartoons, and victory symbols like awards, certificates, degrees, pictures of trophies, and such.

Look for things that inspire or get you fired up, and make you feel good every time you see them. View them and you'll smile, especially when you're having a challenging day or need a lift, and you'll instantly feel better. You'll find this to be indispensable in helping you stay fired up.

It's especially important to include a list of your strengths and positive traits, as they'll help you make your desire for a better life a reality. Take a few minutes now to write down your positive attributes. A good rule of thumb is to list at least 25 qualities that will support you in winning. Number them from 1 to 25 as the ideas pop into your head. Be kind to yourself and acknowledge the wonderful person you are. Once you've finished, read over the list and appreciate yourself. Then put it in your Feel Good Folder.

As a bonus tip, you could also put various items in your Feel Good Folder up at strategic locations around your home and vehicle(s) where you'll see them often.

Staying Fired Up for a Better Life, Tip No. 7—*Keep a "Reward Yourself Jar" and Use It After You've Taken Consistent Action on Your Dream.* For example, say you've given at least five presentations a week, or made five calls to prospects every day. After you've done this great work for a month, reward yourself. That keeps you more consciously invested in the process, helping to keep you fired up, and motivated to keep moving on.

Some people enjoy the reward process so much that they use a Reward Yourself Jar. It's a jar or bottle you fill with strips of paper with rewards written on them. They might say, "Go out to dinner and a movie with your spouse," "Entertain friends," or "Go golfing."

Whatever you consider to be a reward, that's what you write down. Fill the jar with all these goodies and pull one every time you've taken consistent action on your dream for a month. It'll get you fired up to do more and go for it again next month. After a while, you'll have such momentum with your success-inducing habits, you may not need the reward system anymore! You'll be better at blending your fun with your business or profession.

Staying Fired Up for a Better Life, Tip No. 8—*Update Your Action Plan for Dream-Building or Make a New One.* The Action Plan for Dream-Building is a valuable tool for helping you focus on any dream, goal, or objective. Use it any time you have a new dream that you want to be fired up about to make it happen. It will ignite you into taking action.

Staying Fired Up for a Better Life, Tip No. 9—*Create and Expand Your Self-Definition List.* As you move forward toward your dream, you'll be overcoming obstacles and breaking through old fears. Be sure to record these experiences as you track your successes. Pay attention to them. They're important landmarks as you grow and change, and they'll forever transform your self-perception. Refer to them often as examples of how you've grown.

As Oliver Wendell Holmes said…*"The mind, once expanded to the dimensions of a larger idea, never returns to its original size."*

Staying Fired Up for a Better Life, Tip No. 10—*Help Others.* One of the most powerful ways to shift your state from negative to positive is to help others. The key is that it comes from the heart; you're giving and sharing with no attachment to the outcome.

For example, helping others who want a better life can give you a wake-up call that there are a lot of people out there whose lives are not as they'd like them to be, reminding you to appreciate the blessings you already have. You're caring about others, contributing in a positive way, no mater how small. It could be a simple word of encouragement, telling them that they can have a better life, giving them hope. You may be able to help them or refer them to someone who can. A little gesture like that can mean a lot, especially to those who are discouraged in some way. That you're focusing outward to help others will cause you to take your mind off yourself, which will make you feel better. That result alone makes it all worthwhile, helping you to stay fired up.

Staying Fired Up for a Better Life, Tip No. 11—*Ask, Ask, Ask for What You Want.* You'll probably never have anyone more willing than your success coach, leader, or mentor to help you achieve your dreams, but they're not mind readers. Learn to ask specifically for what you want, like Markita Andrews did.

Markita Andrews was an eight-year-old girl whose father had abandoned her and her waitress mother. Both dreamed of traveling around the world, but with their meager income it seemed impossible. That all changed when, at age 13, Markita read in *Girl Scout Magazine* that the scout who sold the most cookies in the country would win an all-expenses-paid trip around the world. Now Markita had a vehicle to realize her dream... and she got fired up. Her burning desire to win this trip led her to create a winning action plan.

Dressed in her uniform every day after school, she would visit people and ask them to invest in her dream by buying one or two dozen boxes of cookies. Pretty soon, with her drive and determination, Markita had sold 3,256 boxes of cookies. She won the trip around the world and since then has sold over 42,000 boxes!

At age 14, she spoke at the international roundtable of the world's top salespeople. Her advice was to ask for the order—ask, ask, ask. True to her motto, she then asked these salespeople to buy her Girl Scout cookies. At that one session, she sold 10,000 boxes, setting a perfect example of how asking for what you want is key to making your dream a reality.

Be clear and specific. Ask for whatever direction or help you need in working toward making your dream a reality; leaders appreciate people who are teachable and earnest in their quest. Imagine your success and picture them assisting you. See yourself as fired up and victorious. Ask your success coach, leader, or mentor to be supportive of you in your pursuit. Guiding you in making it a reality gets them even more fired up, and your example and efforts empower others as well.

Staying Fired Up for a Better Life, Tip No. 12—*Schedule Action Steps for Your Dream in Your Time/Activity Management System or App.* You may currently be doing something else besides living a better life. That's fairly typical and is no obstacle, as long as you take time to focus and work toward it. Bloom where you're planted. Give attention every day to accomplishing your objective. Use your time/activity management system or app to schedule and complete your action steps toward living a better life, one step at a time, doing whatever it takes. That's what winners do.

Staying Fired Up for a Better Life, Tip No. 13—*Attend Seminars Regularly.* Those speaking at seminars are experts in their field. When you're in pursuit of a better life, you'll find it of great value to attend them. They offer a wealth of advantages:

- You'll gain valuable information about what it takes to make your dream for a better life happen.
- You'll meet others who are already successful and living their better life who could be available to help you do the same.
- You'll associate with others who are fired up and taking action, which helps you get and stay motivated.
- You'll listen and take notes, and maybe even purchase an audio or a video of the event or other tools to help you stay fired up.

Staying Fired Up for a Better Life, Tip No. 14—*Counsel with Your Leader, Mentor, or Success Coach.* This is one of the smartest moves you can make in building your business or career. Share your questions and concerns, listen to their advice... then act on it! They'll always have your best interest at heart, and can help you avoid mistakes. Don't try to build your business or profession alone; ask for guidance and suggestions from your success coach, leader, or mentor.

Staying Fired Up for a Better Life, Tip No. 15—*Say Your Affirmations Daily and Make New Ones as Previous Ones Become Reality.* Chapter 17 was all about affirmations. You may have discovered how powerful they are, and how easy they are to do. Use them every day; and once you've achieved the goal of a specific affirmation, be sure to write a new one to take its place. The more you ingrain your success into your subconscious, the more fired up you'll be for living a better life. Create your own set of action options for your affirmations and move on them. Stoke your fire.

Staying Fired Up for a Better Life, Tip No. 16—*Watch Inspiring Movies.* Some great inspirational movies you may want to watch include: *Field of Dreams, The Boy Who Could Fly, Rudy, Angels in the Outfield, Mr. Holland's Opus, The Rookie, October Sky, America's Heart and Soul, Pay It Forward, Heaven Is for Real, Little Miss Sunshine, Moondance Alexander, The Pursuit of Happyness, The Blind Side, Life of Pi, and Saving Mr. Banks.* Perhaps these and others that touch your heart will fire you up for a better life and inspire you to keep moving toward it.

Staying Fired Up for a Better Life Tip, No. 17—*Live in the Present Moment.* It's easy to focus on the future when you're working toward your dream for a better life—and it's necessary to have something to aim for—but you'll experience greater joy and success when you live in the present moment. *The present is the only time in which you can take action.* Be open-minded and committed to taking action now and notice how things happen that support you in achieving your objectives.

Keep agreements for the future and visualize it as fully realized, while enjoying every day as it comes. Remember, *the present is a gift you give to yourself.*

Staying Fired Up for a Better Life, Tip No. 18—*Use Music to Relax, Get Inspired, or Re-Energize.* Music can inspire, motivate, and soothe; choose what supports you. Some like classical for relaxation, movie soundtracks and faith music for inspiration, and fast music or rock and roll to get energized and fired up.

Some songwriters feature positive uplifting messages, reminding us to stay on track, focused and moving on our dream. When you attend a seminar where a band is playing, you can often purchase audios of their inspiring songs. Play them and stay fired up.

Staying Fired Up for a Better Life, Tip No. 19—*Use All Your Resources.* Chapter 11 outlined your resources in detail. Look over that list periodically and determine whether there are some resources available to you which you may not have taken advantage of yet. Stay on track by using the tools your mentor, leader, or success coach recommends—*use their system to help you move on.*

Staying Fired Up for a Better Life, Tip No. 20—*Have Fun and Honor the Child Inside Your Heart.* I'm a big fan of having fun, perhaps because I had a challenging childhood. My husband is one of the best sources for fun ideas, and we schedule it in whenever we can, as long as it doesn't interfere with our objectives.

Again, how you like to have fun is up to you. To stay on track, blend fun with your business activities. For example, at an out-of-town business function, eat at a local restaurant that looks like a fun place that won't break your budget. If you like cars, go to a dealership and test drive one you'd like to own. It's fun looking at the cars and meeting others who like what you do.

Remember, the child inside your heart is a super creative resource for you. You deserve to have fun, not just as a reward for all the work you do, but to stir the embers inside you. Schedule fun activities into your life that are in line with your priorities. Remember the sage advice: *"All work and no play makes Jack a dull boy."*

Staying Fired Up for a Better Life, Tip No. 21—*Exercise in a Way that Supports Your Health.* Maybe you're an exercise enthusiast, or maybe not. Regardless, as you've probably heard time and time again, exercise is one of the keys to good health, feeling good, looking good, and longevity.

Even though I sometimes may not feel like it, I exercise regularly and find it gives me more energy for pursuing my objectives. It helps my blood flow, clears my head, and builds a sound body.

Exercise also enables you to more readily solve problems, as you put your effort into walking, jogging, or whatever exercise you're doing, putting your challenges into perspective. Afterwards you're more relaxed and invigorated, and able to tackle them.

Being healthy requires exercising in ways that support you, giving you greater strength, both physically and mentally. It'll help you stay fired up with the energy to pursue your goals.

Staying Fired Up for a Better Life, Tip No. 22—*Laugh Often.* Have fun with your business or profession. A great sense of humor will help you to be more flexible in dealing with people and challenges. Have you ever said, "Someday we'll look back and laugh at this"? Why wait? Laugh at it now! Ask yourself, "Five years from now, how important will this be?" Probably not too much. Right?

Learn not to take yourself too seriously. Enjoy the process as you're working toward creating a better life. Laugh along the way. Write down some clean jokes and share them while you're talking with others. It'll help "break the ice." So what if you're not yet good at telling jokes. That can be funny in and of itself.

When you're at an out-of-town business function and have some free time, see if there's a comedy club in the hotel or nearby. Get a few good laughs in and you'll be fired up to attend the next session. Spencer and I love to laugh. It helps us to get and stay fired up, especially if negativity tries to creep in. It helps us to revitalize and recommit to our journey of personal and professional growth and achieving our objectives. Laughing can help you too.

Staying Fired Up for a Better Life, Tip No. 23—*Spend Time with Winners.* "Winner" is a subjective term. In sports, it means someone who has played the game and triumphed. A winner in life has a great attitude and an optimistic outlook, and is known for getting things done. A true winner is humble, joyful, always learning, stretching, and growing, and looks for the best in others, rather than criticizing, condemning, or complaining—they're good finders. A winner has setbacks, but when they fall they pick themselves up, dust themselves off, and keep going, forever focused on their goals, while empowering others to do the same.

If you had the choice of associating with a negative-thinking person or a winner, wouldn't you rather spend time with the winner? Which one would encourage and inspire you to move forward? Which one would show appreciation for you and your victories, and care enough to give you honest feedback?

Think about these questions when you decide who to share your dream for a better life with, or even who to spend time with. Negative-thinking people bring others down; stay away from them. Associate with winners. Keep going onward and upward, like a rocket heading to orbit, toward your objectives.

Staying Fired Up for a Better Life, Tip No. 24—*Perform Random Acts of Kindness.* Wanting to make the world a better place, a California artist decided to do unexpected favors for total strangers. Her actions caught on around the country, and the concept of *Random Acts of Kindness* resulted in a bestselling book with those words as its title. Most of the gestures described in the book are small, simple acts, yet make a big difference in the lives of those they touch. Why? As shared in the book...

"At the foundation of every act of kindness is a simple compassionate connection between strangers, who, for a moment, aren't strangers anymore... Kindness, it seems, has the capacity to return us to the very core of our humanity."

Performing a random act of kindness is a great way to get fired up. Something as seemingly inconsequential as purposely leaving change in a store's computer check-out or smiling at or sincerely complimenting a cashier can mean a lot to that person. Who knows? You just might make a friend in the process. It's a feel-good for both of you. As Albert Einstein said...

"The ideals that have lighted my way and, time after time, given me new courage to face life cheerfully, have been Kindness, Beauty, and Truth."

I had a sweet experience with this as a theme one week when a group of us were focusing on kindness. I was in line at the check-out at the grocery store when I started chatting with the woman in front of me. She was obviously from another country and was getting accustomed to the rate of exchange.

I shared how I loved chocolate, as there was a cookbook for sale there with a photo of a chocolate cake featured on the cover. She lit up saying she loved making desserts and experimenting with new recipes, but the price of the cookbook simply wasn't in her budget. As her groceries were being bagged, I bought her the cookbook. To avoid any embarrassment she might have felt, I quickly added, "It's Kindness Week," and told her that I'd love her to have the book. She rewarded me with a great big smile and a joyful thank you.

Little things can mean a lot. Giving, especially when it's unexpected, is such fun and so heartwarming. Do it and find out for yourself. You'll be fired up too.

Staying Fired Up for a Better Life, Tip No. 25—*Have Faith and Believe that You'll Succeed.* Faith is belief in things unseen, and having just a little of it can start you heading toward the better life you're yearning for. That small seed of faith will cause you to start believing that you can really do it. As you make progress, you'll become more inspired to keep going and continue expanding your life experiences.

Your vision of how your life can be comes from faith. It leads to a greater understanding of why you're here and what you're to be doing with your life. Faith is essential for your true happiness, joy, and success—which occur as you're engaged in fulfilling your life's purpose. Go forward in faith as you help others in their quest to live better lives—in line with your purpose—and you can have a better life too.

Staying Fired Up for a Better Life, Tip No. 26—*Celebrate Success and Bring Joy to Others.* In the Walt Disney movie, *Pollyanna*, the main character is a little girl who was orphaned and sent to live with her crusty old aunt. In spite of her harsh surroundings and the strict treatment she receives, Pollyanna maintains a sweet, upbeat disposition and brings joy to the people in her community.

One particularly poignant example of Pollyanna's engaging nature occurred when she visited an elderly woman and her daughter. A negative-thinker, a rather loud and complaining one, she stayed in bed all day, whining and moaning, trying to make everyone else's life miserable too. Pollyanna took the crystal prisms attached to the woman's lamps, hanging them in the sunlit window so that tiny rainbows sparkled throughout the room.

The woman's outlook was magically transformed. The effect was enchanting, as she was delighted with the results. She settled down, stopped whining, and really enjoyed the experience. To Pollyanna, the whole thing was minor and fun; but to the woman it was a very big deal that helped her heal her attitude.

That's spreading joy to others. Your actions may be small and simple, but they can uplift and contribute to someone else's healing process as well as get you and others fired up. One way to give happiness is to celebrate success. Every time you have a win, share it with someone who cares and will be happy for you.

Also celebrate with your business associates and family when they're victorious. Go out to eat or have a cupcake together (with a candle!). Do something inexpensive, fun, and spontaneous. Celebrate all of life's big and little special moments along the way, blending them with your business or profession as much as you can. This will make every day more worthwhile for you and others you care about.

Spreading happiness and joy is a form of service, and it's contagious. The more you share them with others, the more you'll have as well. It's a terrific win-win that helps keep your fire burning.

Staying Fired Up for a Better Life, Tip No. 27—*Share the Dream for a Better Life.* Many people think about this dream and would like it to be so. But typically, they either don't believe they can do it or don't know what to do to make it happen. That's where you come in. Help them bridge the gap between their current situation and their dream of how they'd like to live.

Encourage others to go for their dreams. You could ask them, "How would you describe, in detail, what living a better life would be for you and your family?" Listen closely and let them know that you believe in them and their ability to achieve it...assuring them that they can do it. Cheer them on. Help them get fired up about the good they could make happen for themselves and their loved ones.

This exchange may lead to a new friend. Realize that when you take an interest in others you have the opportunity to get them fired up. Your gifts of enthusiasm and compassion are priceless, as very few people care enough to take an interest in others. Those gifts give you a tremendous advantage in creating new relationships, enabling you to more effectively build your business or profession.

Always share the dream of a better life so you can reach their heart, while inspiring and encouraging them to do it. That's where you can uniquely ignite their fire, so their dream can start coming alive. As a bonus, when you help others get in touch with their dream you'll get even more fired up for your own.

Through it all, you can feel good about knowing that...

In order to enhance your life experience it's essential for you to encourage and empower others to better their lives, while they do the same for still others...and so on down the line.

The List of 27 Tips for
Staying Fired Up for a Better Life

1. Identify What You Truly Want in Your Life
2. Dream-Build Regularly
3. Keep Agreements with Yourself and Others
4. Update Your Dream Collage and Regularly Picture Yourself Living the Life You Want
5. Review Your Daily Success Lists
6. Create a Feel Good Folder and View It Often
7. Keep a "Reward Yourself Jar" and Use It After You've Taken Consistent Action on Your Dream
8. Update Your Action Plan for Dream-Building or Make a New One
9. Create and Expand Your Self-Definition List
10. Help Others
11. Ask, Ask, Ask, for What You Want
12. Schedule Action Steps for Your Dream in Your Time/Activity Management System or App
13. Attend Seminars Regularly
14. Counsel with Your Leader, Mentor, or Success Coach
15. Say Your Affirmations Daily and Make New Ones as Previous Ones Become Reality
16. Watch Inspiring Movies
17. Live in the Present Moment
18. Use Music to Relax, Get Inspired, or Re-Energize
19. Use All Your Resources
20. Have Fun and Honor the Child Inside Your Heart
21. Exercise in a Way that Supports Your Health
22. Laugh Often
23. Spend Time with Winners
24. Perform Random Acts of Kindness
25. Have Faith and Believe that You'll Succeed
26. Celebrate Success and Bring Joy to Others
27. Share the Dream for a Better Life

Chapter 23

Now Go Out and
Make a Bigger Difference
Share Your Fire's Warmth with Others

*"I expect to pass through life but once. If, therefore,
there be any kindness I can show, or any good thing I can
do, let me do it now...as I will not pass this way again."*
William Penn

Are you fired up? You're using the tools in this book and you're moving forward in a positive way. You're motivated, excited, and starting to live a better life, or at least you're moving in that direction. Now what?

I'm Fired Up for a Better Life, Principle No. 32—Make a Bigger Difference

You have an opportunity to spread hope. Go out and plant some "dream seeds" and help keep the dream alive for as many people as you can. Help them get fired up and moving on. Lift others into a more positive experience, putting smiles on their faces, sharing your blessings and enthusiasm. "How do I do that?" you may ask.

It's simple. When you're fired up, you positively influence the lives of those around you. Your excitement helps to uplift others and shake them out of their negativity.

What causes would you like to support more fully? Are you a medical doctor who wants to donate your services, in your country or abroad, to the needy? Do you have a charity you're particularly

148

fond of that you'd like to contribute more money to? Might it be something like the missions Blessed Mother Teresa set up during her lifetime, or an organization that's committed to the cure and elimination of a particular disease? This is a very personal decision. There are many worthy causes in need of support.

Making a bigger difference doesn't have to be a big deal either, and it's often simple and easy. You can make more of a difference every day, no matter what you're doing. Perhaps you just bought a new puppy and, while on a walk, you let little children pet it and giggle. Maybe your favorite baseball team just won and you whistle as you walk down the street, causing others to smile.

You feel happy about your experiences and accomplishments that day and smile at the grocery clerk, calling them by name, and they feel encouraged. You answer the phone and greet a weary caller with a cheerful "Hello, I'm glad you called," and they feel valued and uplifted.

You extend a little kindness to an elderly neighbor by carrying their bags to the door or sweeping the sidewalk, and they feel better knowing somebody cares. You feed the birds and they reward you by singing their songs and visiting daily. You help others take action on their aspirations and they get fired up. Or perhaps you just take a couple of minutes to say hello to a stranger when no one else does, and they appreciate your attention.

All of these are examples of being fired up and touching the lives of others with your warmth. In your own special way, you can ignite the flames of, or empower, other people and make a difference in their lives—many times without even realizing it.

Maria Makes a Bigger Difference

Growing up in a communist country wasn't easy for Maria. Both of her Bulgarian parents worked hard, and her father's strict disciplinarian approach taught her to be strong. At age 14, Maria decided to leave home and go to an English-speaking school. It was there that her dream of being a doctor was born.

Throughout the next several years, she studied and worked with dedication and fervor. She eventually became a respected physician with a specialty in neurology, and was chosen to work at the university hospital. But she fell in love with an American and moved to the United States to share his vision.

Happily married, she nevertheless held on to her longing to practice medicine. After passing the American medical exams, she expected to resume life as a doctor. Months of interviewing taught her how difficult it was for foreign doctors to work in the US. She discovered that the only way for her to succeed was to get a residency at a Boston-area hospital. She made calls, interviewed, observed medical procedures, and made professional contacts wherever possible. Maria got fired up. She took consistent action on her dream and did everything she could to make it a reality.

Two months later, she learned she hadn't been chosen for any of the residencies for which she had applied. Undaunted, she kept on going. That very same day, while observing at a Boston-area hospital, she asked an American co-worker to recommend her to the hiring physician. He did and, later that day, after she had spoken extensively with three physicians, she was hired, triumphing over dozens of other physicians, American and foreign, for the one residency available. She made her dream a reality.

Now she lights up the lives of those she works with and shares her delight at being able to fully live her dream life. She's still fired up and not only makes a bigger difference in the lives of the patients she attends to, but also in the lives of her medical colleagues. They feel the warmth of her fire, enthusiasm, and dedication, reminding them why they originally decided to become doctors. Maria helped them learn to appreciate why they do what they do, which re-ignited their internal flames… and kept her fired up.

Making a Bigger Difference in Mississippi

Osceola McCarty, an uneducated woman from Hattiesburg, Mississippi, worked most of her life as a clothes washer. Even when washing machines became popular, she preferred to wash clothing by hand in a boiling pot to give the highest quality wash. Amazingly, she charged only 50¢ a bundle, which thankfully she was able to increase to $10 a bundle in later years.

With no children of her own, Osceola had the dream of helping African American youth in the area. So she donated her whole life savings of $150,000 to the University of Southern Mississippi for scholarships for black college students. She said, "I want them to have an education. I had to work hard all my life. They can have the chance that I didn't have."

Osceola's generosity astonished her community—so much so that matching funds were raised by area businesses. She was often asked: "Why didn't you spend the money on yourself?" She answers with a big, loving smile, "I *am* spending it on myself." Every graduating student set her fire ablaze. Osceola was fired up and made a bigger difference in the lives of others, leaving a legacy that continues bearing fruit for future generations.

Making a Bigger Difference Through Caring Support

At a speaker's convention I attended years ago, someone told an inspiring story about the Seattle Special Olympics. Nine youngsters, all either physically or mentally challenged, gathered at the start of the 100-yard dash. When the starting pistol sounded, they took off with enthusiasm for winning the race; that is, all except for one boy, who tripped on the asphalt, tumbled, and burst into tears.

As the other contestants heard him cry, one by one, they halted, turned around, and went back to the distraught boy. One girl with Down's bent over him, gave him a kiss and said, "This will make it better." All nine contestants linked arms and walked together over the finish line, getting a standing ovation with cheering that lasted for ten minutes! The crowd was fired up, touched by the caring support these fired-up youngsters demonstrated for each other.

So What Are the Keys to Making a Bigger Difference?

In every one of these examples, each person got fired up about their dream, and in their own unique way reached out and made a bigger difference in the lives of others. Making a bigger difference doesn't have to be all that difficult. You're probably already on track for making a bigger difference, more than you may realize.

In Most Examples of Making a Bigger Difference...

- Action is taken in an upbeat, affirming, caring, encouraging manner.

- This action contributes in a positive way to someone or something, often by inspiring, supporting their healing, sharing ideas, mentoring, success coaching, leading, helping, or creating.

- Enthusiasm is in the air. People are fired up.

The interesting thing about affecting others in a positive way while you're fired up is that you often do it without even being consciously aware of it. This next story illustrates the point.

A Little Boy Lights Up Others

My husband and I were sitting in a pancake restaurant on a rainy Saturday. Many people were allowing the weather to dampen their moods; the atmosphere was quiet and glum. Suddenly, a young boy sauntered in with his parents. After they were seated, he excitedly ran up and down the aisles, giggling all the way. He was fired up about life, eating pancakes, and being with his parents.

His father chased him, laughing, and having fun with his exuberant son. Soon, almost everyone in the restaurant was smiling, and several chuckled, lightened by the child's joyfulness. He lit up the entire restaurant just by being himself, enjoying the experience. Making a positive difference, his fired up-ness gave people permission to smile and laugh, stirring the sparks inside them.

The same is true of you when you share the enthusiasm, happiness, and good nature that result from being fired-up. You're loving what you're doing as you gain exciting new skills in working toward your dream for a better life.

Tips to Help You Make a Bigger Difference

When you're fired up, your enthusiasm and energy can be enormous and make a great impact on others. Here are some tips that can assist you in helping others improve their well-being as you strive to make a bigger difference.

Making a Bigger Difference, Tip No. 1—*Share from Your Heart.* When you're fired up and the flame inside you is burning brightly, *share with others authentically from your heart.* When you're talking about their dream for a better life, let them know it's possible for them to achieve it; that others with all kinds of backgrounds and situations have done it and they can do it too. Understand and share that anyone who has accomplished anything worthwhile has done so in association with others.

Communicate your appreciation of those who believed in you and how they encouraged and guided you every step of the way, or you wouldn't be where you are today. After all, no one can be successful alone. Let others know how grateful you are for all the wonderful people in your life. Give them hope that they can be surrounded by good people, as well, as they work toward making their dream for a better life a reality.

Making a Bigger Difference, Tip No. 2—*Ask Questions and Then Listen.* Remember how, in the beginning of the book, you did the listening exercise with someone? The most important guideline of that activity was to be quiet and not interrupt. You were to give them all the time they needed to share what was on their heart.

Listening skills are essential when you're reaching out and sharing with others. Be sure to ask them to describe what elements would be a part of their better life, what they would like to accomplish, and how they feel about it all. Encourage them to keep talking, while listening carefully to what they have to say. They're likely to appreciate your caring attention, even if they don't tell you so. You'll be able to watch the sparks inside of them ignite, their face reflecting that, as they get fired up right in front of you.

You're taking an interest in others by asking them questions. But when you listen to them you're doing one of the most caring things you can do for them. Make it a regular part of your interactions with others. They'll like being with you and think you're a great conversationalist.

Making a Bigger Difference, Tip No. 3—*Be Unattached to the Outcomes of Sharing and Making a Difference.* To serve means to humbly contribute to the well-being of others by helping them in some way. Always do so, caringly from your heart, with the intention of benefiting all concerned.

Never measure your self-worth based on the outcomes of your good intentions for other people. You're still you, a person of tremendous value, regardless of the results you get with any particular individual—yes, no, maybe, or indifferent.

Remember, other people's reactions, responses, and behaviors are always about themselves. Even though you may want to help someone, they may not want or appreciate your help, or at least not at this time... for whatever reason. Sure, how you treated them could be a factor, but their desires, situations, awareness, maturity, and attitudes, always influence their decisions.

Be content with others living their lives the way *they* choose, letting go of any fears or concerns that they do things *your* way or in your time. They may have to experience more challenges or setbacks before they're motivated enough to get out of their comfort or familiar zones and do something to make a difference in their lives.

When you share or serve, let go of any attachment to a specific outcome. Keep going and growing, doing your personal best, giving it your all. Remember, success is found in the journey. Your growth is a reward, in and of itself, regardless of the outcome!

Making a Bigger Difference, Tip No. 4—*Encourage Others to Pursue Their Own Dream for a Better Life.* You're fired up, working toward living a better life, and taking advantage of all that's available to you to make it a reality. Your attitude is more positive then ever, your life is going better than it ever has, and you're in the process of developing greater success and happiness.

So who could possibly be better than you to help other people with *their* dream for a better life? Share your excitement and, by all means, listen closely to what they're saying, then promote positive, upbeat activities like dream-building and lively seminars.

Show others the way and encourage them, but don't try to force them to do anything. As Dale Carnegie said...

"A man convinced against his will is of the same opinion still."

Believe in everyone, but count on no one. Focus on finding and helping those who are willing to strive for better lives, as you strive in developing yours.

Everyone's own personal history contributes to their perspective. People learn in different ways, and have different proclivities. Give them the space they need, while supporting and encouraging them. Offer suggestions and help if they want it. As the saying goes, "You can't push a rope, but you can gently pull a wet noodle." Since most people are "wet noodles," you can help only those who are ready and willing to be helped.

When you were a kid you attempted to do new things, like riding a bicycle or building a model. You just had to experience it for your-self in order to really learn how to do it and get the satisfaction of mastering it on your own. Your parents may have been tempted to make it easier for you. But the best thing they could have done was to let you "try" it and "fail," over and over again, until you learned and gained your new skill, finally doing it. Growing through the bumps and bruises of the experience yourself was the only way you could truly earn and revel in the victory of accomplishment.

Watching someone else do it simply wasn't enough. So, you did it yourself, the best way you knew how. That's how you learned, grew, and achieved. And that's how adults learn, grow, and achieve too. Share what you know with others—set a good example and empower them to learn, grow, and do it by themselves.

Throughout my experiences in the training business, it's been quite gratifying watching people get fired up and take off in pursuit of their dreams. I've loved watching and learning, listening and experiencing the rich diversity of how the human heart and spirit moves people to action, revealing the value of relentlessly persevering to achieve something worthwhile.

Everyone's current situation impacts everything about their desire for a better life, and the fervor with which they approach its accomplishment. While all true achievers utilize the principles of success; even among those with similar aspirations, no one ever accomplishes them in the exact same length of time, nor does it really matter. They just go until they get it done... and then keep going on to accomplish bigger and better things.

Making a Bigger Difference, Tip No. 5—*Care About Others.* The best way to make a difference in the lives of others is to sincerely care about people. Genuinely share the caring and empathy you have for others. Exhibit kindnesses, go the extra mile, and give others the benefit of the doubt. It requires letting go of any past grievances and forgiving them, as well as stepping forward and doing what needs to be done to help others.

Caring can be shown by lightening up, smiling, laughing, telling a funny story, and being joyful... sharing it all with others. It means reaching out and touching others genuinely in friendship and goodwill. It means being fired up about and sharing what you have to offer with the attitude that it can really make a bigger difference in others' lives.

Celebrate other people's successes, no matter how small, and encourage them when they face disappointments. Remind them of their great potential, while helping them keep their flame alive, stirring their embers if they grow dim, re-igniting their dream to live a better life…as often as necessary.

The "Give Kids the World Village" Non-Profit Resort

The Village was created to help sick children realize their dream of a family vacation. It pays on-site expenses for the kids and their families, from over 70 countries, with more than 250 wish-granting organizations coordinating transportation to central Florida.

While operating a hotel in the Orlando area, Henri Landwirth, a Belgian Holocaust survivor, became passionate about helping sick children. So he founded this foundation to bring them and their families to Disney World, and now also Universal Orlando and Sea World.

Three years later, Henri opened "Kids Village," which today provides housing for 4,000 families on 70 acres. The whimsically themed village includes the Ice Cream Castle, Julie's Safari Theater, the Castle of Miracles, Matthew's Boundless Playground, the Enchanted Carousel, a lake full of fish, a welcome center, the Gingerbread House restaurant, and 141 villas. It's run by a small professional staff, along with volunteers who complete around 1,200 shifts a week. A doctor is always on call to tend to the terminally ill children, aged three to 18.

The foundation's purpose is to bring joy into the lives of the kids and their families, and they consistently do so. "The happiest six days of my child's life" is how one parent described their visit.

Henri clearly demonstrated that one person with a dream to help others make their dreams come true can, indeed, make a bigger difference, while making his own life better in the process. In fact, the Caring Institute honored him as one of the 12 most caring people in America. Henri's life magnificently illustrated Winston Churchill's sage advice…

"We make a living by what we get. We make a life by what we give."

Use Your Fire for a Better Life to Ignite Others' Fires

Your passion, fire, purpose, mission, and fulfillment all give greater meaning to your life. You're brightened and re-energized when you're doing whatever it takes to make a reality of your dream for a better life. Your fire glows brighter every time you share with others that they can do it, too, giving *them* hope, making a positive difference in *their* lives.

When you're fired up for that dream, and encourage and empower others to be and do the same, your fire warms them and your sparks ignite their flames so they can get fired up too. Help them build their enthusiasm so they get fired up to go for their own dream for a better life.

When you, as a fired-up person, befriend others, share what you have to offer, and invite them to become associates or customers, your example and the energized caring atmosphere you provide encourages everyone to get fired up.

It's like lighting another candle from your own—doubling the fire, light, and heat—which fires you up even more! Then as soon as the person holding the second candle lights a third person's candle, the fire, light, and heat triples...and so on. Lighting another's flame takes nothing from your flame; it simply multiplies its effectiveness.

Since you were born with pure potential, as a fired-up person you *can* overcome any obstacle, persisting as you incrementally better your life. Ignite the fire inside, stay fired up, and keep moving. Strive for that dream for a better life, while championing the cause of empowering others to be fired up to do the same... and so on.

You now have the knowledge and wisdom, as well as the tools, to get and stay fired up. So it's now time to start shouting, *"I'm fired up for a better life!"*; meaning it with all your heart and soul, as you go forward in doing whatever it takes in making your better life a reality.

You Can Do It!

When you're fired up for a better life you create the atmosphere for great things to happen... even miracles! Your fire can warm those you invite to get closer to you, igniting their flames. This can excite them to become customers or associates and get fired up for better lives of their own, and on down the line. As Helen Keller said...

"Alone we can do so little; together we can do so much."

In concert with others you can achieve even more than you may now think possible.

I'm Fired Up for a Better Life—The Creed

Inside of me is the fire of life—my passion, purpose, mission, and fulfillment, which give my life meaning. It burns brightly as I constantly strive to better my life, using my imagination to get clear about what I really want to accomplish, regularly visualizing it as an evolving life-long journey.

As a fired up person, I'm improving my life all the time. I dream-build, connect with the right people, and diligently work toward realizing my aspirations. I seek the wisdom and assistance of others who are where I want to be, and express my appreciation for their help and taking an interest in me. I'm thankful for the desire to grow and become the best I can be, as I gain the ability to make my better life a reality.

As a fired up person, I use the career- or business-building tools my leader, mentor, or success coach recommends, care for my health, use my time wisely, manage my money well, and get out of debt. I laugh often and watch inspiring movies. I read from a positive book and listen to an educational or motivational audio every day. I attend live seminars, webinars, and other business-related activities, as suggested by my mentor, leader, or success coach. I grow and develop personally and professionally every day.

As a fired up person, I say my affirmations daily. I overcome all obstacles and keep going no matter what, doing whatever it takes to achieve my dreams, goals, and objectives. I focus on my dream collage daily, stoking my fire for creating a better life.

As a fired up person, I pursue my dream for a better life with passion, persistence, and a positive vision of the outcome. I regularly associate with people who are more successful then I am, and I empower others to do the same. I use every experience, positive or negative, as an opportunity to learn, grow, and move on. Staying fired up keeps me motivated to strive for a better life and make a bigger difference, as I share my enthusiasm and what I have to offer with everyone I know and meet. *I'm fired up for a better life!*

—THE END—

**Or could this be your fired-up path to
a brighter tomorrow; an exciting new beginning...**
for you and those you care about?

159

Who Is Anne Whiting?

Anne Whiting is a speaker, trainer, and author. Thirty-one years ago she founded her own advertising and training agency, and continues on as president and creative director. Her trademark qualities are genuine enthusiasm and the ability to get people fired up to take action.

Anne began her professional career as an educator, and is still actively involved with youth through organizations like Project Safeguard and the YMCA. A keynote motivational speaker and trainer for general adult audiences, associations, conventions, organizations, and corporations, she is also a member of the National Speaker's Association.

Anne lives with her husband Spencer and their two cats and loves to sail, travel, write, dance, and entertain. Her passion is to help people to be more successful and live a better life.